Own Goal!

Own Goal!

How Egotism and Greed
are Destroying Football

SIMON FREEMAN

ORION

The right of Simon Freeman to be identified as the author
of this work has been asserted by him in accordance with
the Copyright, Designs and Patents Act 1988.

First published in Great Britain in 2000 by
Orion Media
An imprint of Orion Books Ltd
Orion House, 5 Upper St Martin's Lane,
London WC2H 9EA

A CIP catalogue record for this book
is available from the British Library

Typeset by Deltatype, Birkenhead, Wirral
Printed in Great Britain by
Clays Ltd, St Ives plc

Contents

To Gillian

I would like to thank Jo Bowlby, my agent, and Trevor Dolby, of Orion Books, for their support. Allan and Elsie Corkindale were helpful and entertaining, although they knew that I did not share their enthusiasm for Manchester United. Their daughter, Gillian Cribbs, was an inspiration and was always ready to listen to my memories of the great days at Brighton and Hove Albion and my theories on what was wrong with football today, despite her lifelong loathing of the sport. Finally, I must thank my mother for her encouragement.

Simon Freeman
London
May 2000

Chapter One

Snapshots

A glorious August evening and the Hillgate pub near my home in Notting Hill, west London, has unfurled the screen for Sky Sport's latest feast of football, the match between Aston Villa and West Ham. When Sky started showing live football a few years ago the Hillgate was always packed on match days but tonight it is almost empty, despite the fact that West Ham are a London team and both sides are renowned for their free-flowing, imaginative play. Neither is a member of the elite of the Premier League – Manchester United, Arsenal and Chelsea – giants which turn over many tens of millions of pounds a year. Aston Villa, from Birmingham, could join this band one day, because they draw support from the West Midlands urban sprawl, but West Ham are based in the working-class East End and will always be a Premier League also-ran.

I am here because I have followed West Ham since school, where my closest friend, Richard, was the cousin of Trevor Brooking, one of West Ham's and England's finest players. After a kickabout one lunchtime at school many years ago, Richard told me that Trevor intended to give up football if he was not in the first team by the time he was eighteen. Trevor made it but Richard did not; he died of cancer in his early twenties.

I am the only person in the Hillgate this evening who is watching the crumpled screen and listening to the shrieking commentators and the thick sound effects; biff, bang, thwack –

every kick and tackle is picked up by Sky's microphones to make the viewers feel as if they are in Villa Park.

The Hillgate is more crowded for the Sunday afternoon clash at Highbury between Arsenal and Manchester United, but there are still only a couple of dozen people. Most are men, drinking pints. Football is supposed to have become middle class but this is the traditional working-class audience. The majority are more interested in their beer than the game and the few who do watch are United fans, which emphasises the fact that United are an international brand name, not a mere football club from the richest city in the country outside London.

There is a handful of women, however, including an elegant young woman who is studying a travel book on Brazil. She looks up and applauds when United score but then returns to her book. Football's blow-dried, designer-stubbled millionaires have attracted many women to the game but few care about what happens on the field, which suggests to me, politically incorrect though it may be, that top-class football is eye candy for them, the female equivalent of *Baywatch*, an American television programme featuring models in tiny swimsuits pretending to be lifeguards. Many of the players on show are foreign, drawn to England by salaries of £25,000 and more a week, after tax – plus free houses, cars and as many minutes of mobile phone time as they can use.

The game is fast but no more skilful or exciting than it was twenty years ago when teams of English, Scots, Welsh and Irish peopled the First Division, and Europe was a snapshop of clichés of cheating Italians, flimsy French and robotic Germans. Sky's commentators cannot say this, of course, and babble on as if the game is a classic, in between reminding viewers to tune in again for more football during the week.

Football's expansion is infinite and inexorable. Once it was edited highlights late at night on BBC television (usually on a Saturday) and perhaps a match the following day between bumbling local teams on a regional station. But now there is Sky and a gaggle of satellite and digital competitors. Soon every major club will have its own station, which will mean that Manchester United fans in Torquay or Los Angeles will be able to track their team in the Premier League, domestic cups (if the club thinks these are worth entering) and assorted European, super-European and intercontinental competitions, without budging from their living-room sofas. Television will invent more gimmicks because these will generate income. The fan who can only watch a match through the traditional cameras will be a member of a viewing underclass. Already there is 'interaction' with the set: with Sky digital you can select camera angles, and order replays and statistics. Next, viewers will be able to access conversations between referees, players and assistant referees. Then, when the public is bored with that, tiny microphones will be attached to players. Eventually, mini cameras will be attached to the players and, possibly, to the ball. Microphones and cameras will invade the dugout, where managers, coaches and substitutes sit; finally, after squeals of protest from clubs about giving away secrets – this will be silenced by the amount of money offered – television cameras will be fitted in dressing rooms.

More, more, more. More money for players, managers, agents, sponsors, shareholders, football journalists, newspapers, magazines and television. The fans, meanwhile, have become customers, consumers, clients. They are expected to spend ever-increasing amounts of money – on seats, television and 'merchandise', which is football-speak for junk embossed with a club crest. They are told that they are part of this exciting new world, but they are not; they are outsiders, whose only role is to hand over money.

Football grew because it was the working man's escape from the drudgery of work. In the 1980s it became the focus for the violent and dispossessed; the set-piece battles in town centres around the country every Saturday between gangs were tribal but also reflected the breakdown of industrial society. During the premier-ship of Margaret Thatcher football was heading towards oblivion, like the coal mines, the shipyards and the steel works, the decaying relics of the old Britain. Then came the catastrophes in 1985 which, paradoxically, saved football. The deaths at Bradford City and the Heysel Stadium in Brussels forced the sport to confront what it had become: the symbol of everything that was rotten about post-war, post-colonial, post-industrial Britain. In April 1989 came the disaster at Hillsborough, when ninety-five people were crushed at the start of an FA Cup semi-final, which forced football to accept that it had to modernise or perish. The rebuilding, of attitudes as well as stadia, began but football remained working class and unfashionable.

All this changed in the World Cup in Italy in the summer of 1990, when the country was entranced by the new soccer. The players were tanned, lithe, eloquent. The crowds were excited and peaceful. The stadia were design masterpieces. And there was Paul Gascoigne: the idiot-genius whose tears during England's semi-final with Germany symbolised football's new glamour. The sport which Thatcher had consigned to the rubbish bin of history was not only saved that summer; it was transformed into a multimillion pound industry.

A steaming hot day in London in August 1999 and England are playing Luxembourg at Wembley. They have to win to stand any chance of qualifying for the play-offs for the championship to be held in summer 2000 in Holland and Belgium. The press have been frothing over the game, as if Luxembourg are Brazil rather than a collection of podgy painters, decorators and bank clerks, and this is the World Cup Final. The crowd reveals that football remains a resolutely male sport watched by those whose education, jobs and income place them in the C and D social classes. Fans overflow from the pubs around the stadium. The atmosphere is good-natured but you sense that it would not take much to detonate them because, beneath the smiles and the jokes about Alan Shearer, there is the anger of people whose working lives are miserable. Football is escape, an opportunity to lash out, verbally or physically. Many are wearing – draped over their shoulders or tucked into their jeans or shorts, over sagging white flesh – ghastly, nylon England replica shirts.

The concourse of the stadium is thick with the stench of over-priced hot dogs, hamburgers, chips – which the fans stuff down to soak up the beer and lager. There are some children but hardly any women. This is not the middle-class family sport suggested by surveys.

Wembley's twin towers are instantly recognisable around the world but the stadium itself is a disgrace. Built in the early 1920s, its only virtue is the pitch, a sweeping, smooth billiard table; but everything else about the place is decrepit. The lavatories look as if they have been shipped in from the Third World. Many fans insist on standing during the game, partly because it is more exciting and partly because they cannot tolerate the discomfort of the little bits of plastic laughably described as seats.

The match is an embarrassment. Luxembourg are as useful as a semi-professional team which trains twice a week in the local pub car park. By half-time the score is 5-0 and England give up in the second half. Only one player, thirty-seven-year-old full back Stuart Pearce, is interested, because he knows that he will never play again for his country at Wembley.

It says much about football today that this match has taken place. Euro 2000 has expanded to include the new nations of Central and Eastern Europe, even though many field teams which would struggle on Wormwood Scrubs on a Sunday morning. But more teams mean more matches which means more money for everyone – national associations, the European governing body, UEFA and television. This also intensifies the conflict between the major clubs, whose players are expected to turn out in these games, and the national associations. There has always been tension between club and country but country usually won – because competitions like the World Cup mattered and because players

5

were judged by their performances in these events – but the balance has shifted now; today, the games between the major clubs matter more than internationals.

Newspapers find this perplexing because the England team, apparently always in crisis, always disappointing, helps them fill their pages, while television pays millions for the rights to screen these internationals. So everyone pretends that this is high-class sporting drama. The press box at Wembley – a misnomer because the 'box' is nothing more than seats in a stand, with glass-fronted booths at the back for television – is packed. Radio commentators yell into their microphones – AND IT'S ENGLAND ALL THE WAY – television pundits debate whether Keegan will pull it off in Poland the following week and writers tap away on their laptops. The story of the day, which will keep the media going until Wednesday's game in Warsaw, is Newcastle's Alan Shearer: he scores a hat trick, including a penalty, but the journalists agree that he has lost the pace and manoeuvrability which made him a special centre forward.

The following Wednesday, it seems that they are right. England draw with Poland and confirm that the Premier League's English players are no better than their predecessors, who earned three, not three hundred, times the average salary. Their over-inflated status is exemplified by Shearer, who spends the match thrusting his backside and elbows into the Poles. Yet he is paid £40,000 a week by Newcastle and is reportedly worth millions on the transfer market.

It seems today that everyone has always loved football. Anyone who needs public approval – politicians, pop singers, novelists, chefs – claims to be a lifelong fan. A few admit to supporting one of the giants but most swear allegiance to the struggling club back home in Halifax, Wigan or Barrow. Some are genuine: when Rod Stewart juggled a ball on stage at a concert it was obvious that he would have exchanged the money and the fame for a few years as a

Fourth Division pro, but most of these 'celebrities' know little about the game.

Amongst the hundreds of football web sites on the Internet there is one listing the celebrities who claim to be passionate about football. Taking their lead from Tony Blair, the Prime Minister, and his chief spin doctor, Alistair Campbell (to be fair to Campbell he is a genuine fan, who has been obsessed with his club, Burnley, since he was a boy) ambitious Labour Party politicians have begun to embrace football – and to kick or head a ball whenever a photographer or television camera is present. Public figures have always known that they must endorse contemporary moralities and fashions – Christianity, the Empire, anti-Communism – but today it is football.

A bleak autumn night and European football is on television again. This time West Ham are playing away against a Romanian team in the UEFA cup. The pitch looks as if it has been transplanted from Hackney Marshes. The stadium is an ancient concrete bowl, of the sort found in England in the 1930s. There are about 12,000 spectators, including several thousand West Ham fans. This is about the average for a top of the table English Second Division club. The football is of the same standard, too.

The commentator tries to inject excitement – he keeps screaming that the stadium is a cauldron of hate – but we have seen too many games like this, which we are supposed to salivate over because *this is Europe*. The same night Leeds beat a mediocre Swiss side at home, in a match of interest only to committed locals, and Newcastle defeat a team in Zürich in front of 9,500 people. The previous evening Chelsea went to Istanbul where the tabloid press claimed they would be in mortal danger from the evil Turks; by the time they scored their fifth goal most of the crowd had gone home, presumably to beat up their wives if the press caricatures were to be believed. The night before both Arsenal and Manchester United performed, badly, in the premier competition, the UEFA Champions' League. But none of the results are important because

UEFA has invented competitions from which only the spectacularly inept can be eliminated in the early rounds.

In my youth I was good but not nearly good enough. I was small, fast and combative. At grammar school I lived for the lunch hour, when we staged eleven-a-side games on the playing fields, and came back for lessons in the afternoon drenched with sweat but happy. In those days, when schools had masters who sacrificed their leisure to run sports teams, we had sides for the U12s, U14s and so on, up to the First XI, who were gods. We played other schools, home and away, when we would travel on coaches and imagine that we were professionals.

Today many state schools lack the money – and teachers willing to give up their weekends – to organise competitive football. The best players are creamed off by the Football Association's 'academies' which are attached to professional clubs. Other promising players turn out for the junior teams of non-league or amateur clubs. Instead of learning how to be total footballers, who can tackle, pass, dribble and shoot with both feet, they are told, aged eight, that they are, say, a full back or a striker. They play on full-size pitches, being screamed at by 'coaches' and parents. At an age when they should be enjoying themselves and experimenting with skills and positions they are told that winning is all that matters. The pundits say that, obviously, we cannot copy Brazil, where football is woven into the fabric of life, but we can learn from countries such as Holland, where the emphasis is on enjoyment and skill for children, not winning some meaningless league.

Slowly age takes its toll. One day you can go past an opponent, the next you feel as if your legs are made of lead. Injuries linger. But you cannot give up the Saturday or Sunday match. Then the team begins to fall apart. The keeper's wife says that he has to go shopping, or else. The midfield general has a new job in New York.

The striker's GP warns him that his knees will pack up completely if he continues playing.

In spring 1999 I became a football columnist for the Sunday newspaper in Glasgow which employed me as its London editor, covering national and international affairs from a desk close to the cut-price electronics shops in Tottenham Court Road.

Glaswegians were not interested in my reflections on racism in the Metropolitan Police, gun control in the United States or massacres in Central Africa, but football was different. Of course they cared most about their own teams, Rangers and Celtic, but, like fans everywhere, they were not parochial. So they devoured stories on the future of Wembley Stadium, Glenn Hoddle's demise as England manager and South Africa's bid to stage the World Cup in 2006.

Then Scotland were drawn to play England, home and away, to decide who would qualify for the European Championship in Holland and Belgium the following summer. It was front page news in Scotland. This was partly because Scots always treated a match against England as if it were the World Cup Final but it was also about devolution. Amid excited comparisons with the new nations of Eastern Europe and the old Soviet Union, Scots had just elected a parliament; they were not happy when it became clear that it had the limited powers and feeble personalities of a county council and blamed the English for tricking them. Now they wanted their football team to wreak revenge.

I took the tube to Heathrow to attend the press conference at the Marriott Hotel. Arranged by the Nationwide Building Society, this was to celebrate the draw by UEFA. By an unfortunate coincidence the Nationwide sponsors both teams but, determined to turn this to its advantage, its public relations maestros have summoned Kevin Keegan and Craig Brown, Scotland's manager, to meet the media.

Both men are small and wear baggy tracksuit tops emblazoned with the Nationwide logo. Keegan has put on a few pounds since he retired after a glittering career with Liverpool, Hamburg, Southampton and Newcastle, but still has the tight skin and sheen of the professional athlete. Brown, however, is crumpled, as befits a middle-aged former teacher. There are dozens of reporters, photographers and camera crews. It does not matter that neither man has anything interesting to say: football is big news.

Keegan and Brown endure several hours of questioning. While Keegan is mouthing platitudes to reporters from the Sunday newspapers, Brown is chuntering to camera crews from football 'specials'; then they switch positions and start again. Listening to Keegan I feel sorry for him, despite his salary of around £900,000. He is friendly and cracks jokes as he dodges loaded questions but soon he is repeating himself – 'How, err, important, is this game, Kevin?' 'I mean, it's a massive game, isn't it, for both teams, but it's important that we don't let the pressure get to us.' Brown, paid about £190,000 a year, is Einstein compared with Keegan, but that does not mean he has anything to say either; he just says nothing more intelligently. He compliments Keegan and England frequently; the game will be tough but his boys are 'up for it', and that is it, though my colleagues scribble busily throughout, as if real issues are being addressed.

I cannot blame Keegan or Brown. There is just not enough to say about the matches. You could ask about tactics, selection, preparation and pressure; you could expand into some general points, such as the impact of so many foreigners on the domestic game and that is it. But the media demands controversies and rows.

Long ago a big match involving the England team emptied the streets and shops of London. The entire capital gathered around television sets on a summer evening in 1990 when England played West Germany in the semi-final of the World Cup in Italy; and in 1966 the whole country vanished into their living rooms to watch England win the World Cup in flickering black and white. But on a dull, cold Saturday afternoon in November 1999, London carries on shopping and eating and going to the cinema, as if the match between Scotland and England is not happening. Pubs that unfurl their Sky Sports screens are busier than usual but otherwise the game at Hampden Park has as much mass appeal as the mixed doubles final at Wimbledon.

There are many reasons for this. First, despite the efforts of Rupert Murdoch to convince us that life consists of multi-channel choice, most people have not subscribed to Sky; if the game were broadcast live on terrestrial television, many of those who pass the afternoon spending more than they can afford would stay at home. The BBC's screening of the match, in full, immediately after the final whistle is both silly and irrelevant. Or perhaps, after all, the average football fan is not as stupid as the media thinks. Despite the absurd media hype that this is the most important football confrontation in history, most fans probably realise that what is being offered is a match between two average-to-poor sides. It might be a sign that people are sick of televised football; or it might be an indication that, in this era of the super-club, no one cares about the England team until – and if – it reaches the final stages of a major championship.

It might be a demonstration of maturity. The old rivalry between England and Scotland, admittedly always more intense north of the border, once automatically injected drama into these fixtures. But all this seems old fashioned late in 1999, as the most violent century in history staggers to a close.

But Scotland are not so laid back. Driven on by the dwarves of the Scottish media – who think that they are the power elite of a new nation – the yobs who support Protestant Rangers and Catholic Celtic temporarily shelve their ancient religious hatreds and turn on the English fans who travel to Scotland.

In the Hillgate the hard-drinking regulars are joined by young City professionals in fleece jackets and designer jeans and their pretty trust-fund girlfriends, who have read their morning papers and decided that this is an event not to be missed. Judging by the comments ('Is that David Beckham?' one young woman asks her boyfriend as Paul Scholes is booked after celebrating his first goal with an inflammatory gesture), however, few of the audience know much about football.

For the first twenty minutes, as Scotland waste chance after chance, the game is gripping. Then Scholes scores. A few people cheer, without much enthusiasm: this is England, not Manchester United, Chelsea or Arsenal. Scotland pour forward but it is passionless, in contrast to the frenzied opening; by now the pub senses that we had been cheated: the Scots are ordinary players doing their best but they are definitely not stoked up with the kind of fervour which the media has been gabbling about all week. We are watching the equivalent of a match between two struggling Premier League teams, who cannot afford the foreigners who have transformed football here.

England are untroubled. Paul Ince snarls and swears. Alan Shearer thrusts his large backside into defenders. David Beckham is languid, tossing his hair back, as if he is auditioning to replace David Ginola, the Frenchman with long, thick hair who played for Spurs, in between modelling on teleivision as a shampoo icon. Jamie Redknapp of Liverpool looks as if he is being reeled by an invisible line into the centre of the midfield from his unaccustomed position on the left. The Spanish referee keeps flashing his yellow card, presumably to remind the players that they are supposed to be taking this seriously, but then Manchester United's David Beckham and Paul Scholes kill the match.

We have been told that Craig Brown has spent hours preparing his players for Beckham's free kicks. Brown might well be a master tactician but a tactician can only hope that his players remember what he has told them when they leave the dressing room; Scotland's players obviously lack the mental equipment to store simple instructions. England win 2-0.

Beckham's free kick swung in fast but would have been dealt with ninety-nine times out of a hundred by a Premier League defence. But Scotland stood and watched, as little Scholes ran in unmarked from the edge of the penalty area. He headed the ball into Scotland's net and the game was over.

Snapshots

The second half drifted past, as the pub emptied and the remained turned away to concentrate on their beer and Sky's commentators shouted louder and louder in an atte. hold the viewers but it was hopeless and by the time the game ended most people were not watching.

I do not want to romanticise the past, like old buffers in pubs who say that conscription was a damned good thing. There is much that is better about football today, just as there is about life. This book is about the transformation of a game which was the bedrock of cities and towns into a multimillion, multinational industry; it is also about the crisis which football faces, born of greed and nurtured by stupidity.

To compete, clubs pay staggering salaries to ordinary players, financed by television deals, fans and a host of business ventures. Foreign players pour in, eager to share in the cash bonanza. Teams routinely field more foreigners than locals, which further erodes the link between club and community.

Only a few clubs can afford to pay £30,000 a week to an indifferent player with a drink problem. Meanwhile, the pursuing pack of clubs are spending more and more, and falling further into debt. The clubs in the First, Second and Third Divisions once relied on transfer fees to balance their books, but the Premier League now shops abroad because it is cheaper and the players are more glamorous. Freedom of contract means that players can move from a club whenever their agents sniff bigger pay packets.

Fast forward a few years. The Premier League is dominated by a handful of cash-rich giants. The rest of the division exists to make up the numbers. Many clubs in the lower divisions are close to bankruptcy because fans prefer to watch top teams on television. Go forward a few more years. The Premier League is an irrelevance. The major clubs concentrate on the European Super League and the World Championship. They do not even enter the FA Cup.

Then fashion changes and football becomes naff. Rupert

Own Goal!

Murdoch has died and his empire has fractured. Sky's audience for live football has shrunk and the station can no longer afford to pay hundreds of millions of pounds to broadcast games. The giant clubs can survive this because they are now corporations, but the rest of the professional game implodes. Clubs become part-time or fold. But no one cares.

A few days after the Hampden Park non-event, England and Scotland meet again at Wembley. It is a cold night but more than 70,000 people, including a few thousand Scots in kilts and replica shirts, pack into this ageing stadium, which should have been torn down long ago, for what is supposed to be a celebration of English superiority.

Tonight, however, the Scots rediscover the passion that has traditionally fuelled their encounters with the Auld Enemy. At half-time they lead 1-0 and seem destined to score again in the second half and force extra time. The Scots revel in their role as plucky and oppressed minnows but a second goal, perhaps leading to a famous victory and qualification for Euro 2000, is not part of the script; they run and run but they seem to want to return home as brave losers. Alan Shearer, his best days gone, hustles around the pitch, impersonating a footballer. He thrashes one chance high over the bar and then, frustrated that his body can no longer do what his mind orders, clatters into the Scottish goalkeeper. Ron Atkinson, the ex-manager of many top clubs, who is famous for his perma-tan, sunglasses and love of good champagne, has a new career as a television pundit, and growls happily. Ah, he says as the referee signals a foul, in the great old days of Nat Lofthouse (Bolton's battering ram centre forward who scored thirty goals for England in the 1950s), that would have been a fair challenge. Keegan shivers on the touchline in his designer tracksuit while Brown grins nervously at the thought of his team travelling to Holland and Belgium to be humiliated in Euro 2000.

Because this is an England match at Wembley, it is televised live on ITV – it requires a Ph.D in marketing to understand the allocation of television rights in football – which means that the pubs in Notting Hill only have to cope with their regulars. But ITV knows that it has to bolster its schedules tonight and sandwiches the England game between two editions of the quiz show *Who Wants to Be a Millionare?*, an extraordinarily successful programme in which contestants answer multiple-chance questions in a doomed effort to win a £1 million jackpot.

The match is more exciting than the Hampden game, but only because Scotland try so hard. Meanwhile, the commentators, in between praising Scottish courage, trailer forthcoming attractions on ITV: great European action with Manchester United and Chelsea, as well as Worthington Cup specials.

England win but football loses. The myth of the Premier Leagues in England and Scotland is exposed again; these players are millionaires but this does not make them better than their predecessors. David Beckham has designer stubble, earns the equivalent of a lottery win every six months and is married to a Spice Girl but has no more talent than those long-forgotten midfielders who disappeared from the game and became publicans, hod carriers or postmen after they had retired.

The media is delighted that England have performed so abysmally against Scotland. Good, or, even worse, average, performances are boring but disasters have to be analysed. Thus, the match inspires tens of thousands of words berating the greed of today's Premier League stars, the debilitating impact of so many foreigners at major clubs, the incompetence of the Football Association in appointing Keegan, who was acclaimed as a saviour a few months earlier and so on. A few days later Keegan is treated like a war criminal by the press after an England player reveals that a few members of the squad had stayed up after the first match at Hampden to watch a world heavyweight title fight being televised from the States. But he fights back, with a dignity that is rare in football. The problem is not late night boxing but the fact that his team played badly. He does not know why so many good players were so awful but it is his job to find out and ensure that it does not happen again. He argues, rightly, that it will only take one good performance for the media to acclaim his team as potential European champions. But measured common sense like this does not make for headlines and journalists pour out their analyses into the *real* reasons for the defeat.

And so the football circus – players, managers, clubs, broadcasters, pundits, agents, sponsors and assorted hangers-on – rolls on, its protagonists locked in a profitable embrace, squabbling and feuding, but united in their desire to make as much money as possible before the public comes to its senses and realises that everything – from the excellence of the Premier League to controversies about late nights by the England squad – is a con.

These are the truths about football today:

• The Premier League consists of a few giants which generate hundreds of millions of pounds a year; the rest are there to make up the numbers.
• The gulf is widening so fast that future champions will always be drawn from this super-elite. The others do not have the money to buy the players who can compete.
• The giants of England – and the rest of Europe – have forced UEFA to expand the European Cup, which used to be a knockout competition between the champions of Europe's domestic leagues. The new Champions' League is a European super-league, which was not supposed to happen. But it will fail. The fans, in Manchester, London, Madrid, Barcelona, Marseilles, Milan and Rome and elsewhere, loved 'European nights' because they were special. The games were cultural clashes, between, say, muscular but technically inept British or Irish teams and temperamentally suspect but artistic Spaniards. This was crude national stereotyping but it gave a frisson to these matches. Fans do not want regular matches between super-clubs; they are sustained by local pride, which means Liverpool against Manchester United, AC Milan against Inter Milan, Real Madrid against

Athletico Madrid. The Champions' Cup – or, as it should be known, the Champions-Plus-Also-Rans Cup – is shadowed by the UEFA Cup, which has absorbed the Cup Winners' Cup. And, finally, there is the curious beast known as the Inter-Toto Cup, which feeds three teams into the UEFA Cup.

- Only clubs with large squads will be able to compete in these competitions. So, even if a medium-sized Premiership club, such as West Ham, squeezes into the Champions' League it will implode under the pressure of too many matches.

- The also-rans of the Premier League will ally with the once-great clubs of the First Division – like Wolves and Nottingham Forest – to form Division Two of the Premier League. The remaining clubs, the minnows of the First, Second and Third Divisions, will drift into semi-professionalism or extinction.

- Television will control the game. As it tightens its grip it will move live football on to subscription channels. It will introduce new gimmicks to make the game more compelling. Already we have Sky's 'interactive' digital service: in future, as viewers become bored with this, television will utilise new technology. But there is a limit to the dramatisation of twenty-two men kicking a football.

- Crowds are essential to television but fans are drifting away, forced out by ever-increasing ticket prices. To ensure that televised games have 'atmosphere', admission charges will fall, which, in turn, means that television will have to pay more for rights.

- The middle classes will tire of football outside the luxurious stadia of the top Premier League clubs.

- Football, like boxing, once offered an escape for the working classes but prosperity means that youngsters today spend their free time playing computer games or watching multi-channel television. State schools lack the facilities and the staff to organise competitive sports. Already managers are complaining about the dearth of young talent.

17

Own Goal!

Many people argue that it is too late to stop the disintegration of professional football. They say that there is no point even trying because football reflects society. But there *is* an alternative view: societies which only judge success in financial terms are doomed. Football, like any sport, must show that life is not only about making money.

In the United States, the home of ultimate me-me-me capitalism, governing bodies in major sports (basketball, baseball and American football in particular) have imposed caps on clubs' salary bills and have established a system, known as the draft, which ensures that the brightest young talent from colleges or elsewhere gets to some of the weaker clubs, thus ensuring that leagues remain competitive. Unfortunately, for many reasons, this could not happen in British football.

The days when football was based on an industrialised working-class culture have gone. Now it is a branch of show business and fashion and will probably remain so. Football should remember what happened when boxing forgot its roots – it became a pay-as-you-view minority sport, of limited interest. Football's governing bodies should act now to guarantee competition between clubs in England and, indeed throughout Europe, in response to fans' wishes.

The governing bodies should limit the number of games shown on television. They should try to limit the number of cut-price foreign players in our league, though European Union law makes this difficult, and probably impossible. They should balance the short-term rewards of huge deals with subscription channels against the long-term damage of removing football from licensed terrestrial channels. And, finally, they should invest money in youth football to attract children to the game; and they should limit wages to save clubs from bankruptcy.

Chapter Two

The Fans

Allan Corkindale has been following Manchester United since he was eleven. He was born and educated in Manchester and has lived there all his life. As a young civil servant he was marked out for promotion, but he turned down the opportunity, because that would have meant leaving United. He never misses a home game. Despite a recent major heart operation, and now in his mid-sixties, he travelled by charter flight to Barcelona to watch United win the Champions' League in 1999. He took his wife, Elsie, who is only marginally less passionate about United, to Monaco to watch United play Lazio in a match whose only purpose was to make money. When he came home I asked him if he minded that United had treated Monaco as a practice session; he frowned, as if he was a priest who had been asked to deny God.

Allan is the father of Gillian, a close friend. I met him in the early 1990s and recall him sitting glumly in her living room in south London after tea, wondering what he should say to me; most of her friends were Oxbridge graduates who had never heard of Pele. I asked if he thought Peter Schmeichel, United's Danish goalkeeper, was better than Peter Shilton, who had played more than a hundred and twenty-five matches for England. He took another sandwich from the tray, ruminated and then said that, on balance, he did. He told me that he had once bumped into Schmeichel outside Old Trafford, which reminded him of the time when, as a boy, he had sat next to a United player on the bus. But that was more than fifty years ago and it couldn't happen today which was a shame because it had been marvellous to be so close to an idol. I agreed and said that United players now own garages full of luxury cars and would not dream of travelling on public transport.

We talked about the Busby Babes, Bobby Charlton, Denis Law, Ryan Giggs and Alex Ferguson. Allan is an intelligent and well-read man and knew that I was right when I said that football is no more exciting than it was in the past and that, though modern players might be fitter and tactically more sophisticated, the game does not produce stars like George Best, who could fill a stadium. Ah well, yes, he said reluctantly, as if criticising United to a non-believer like me was a mortal sin.

Once I stayed at his home. As a treat he took me to watch an evening match at Old Trafford, a youth team cup final with Leeds, along with about 25,000 others. Just look at the size of the crowd, he said proudly, as if the multinational business which is Manchester United cared what he thought. Whenever United reached a cup final at Wembley, which was often, he would come to London. Gillian would organise visits to the theatre and to restaurants but Allan could not disguise the fact that what mattered was the game. On the night before the big day he would fret about transport – should he go by Underground, how long would it take, where should he get off? – and next morning would put on his ancient United replica shirt underneath his sweater, in defiance of his daughter who detests football and who cannot understand why her parents waste their money watching odious young men kicking a ball around a field.

A few years later he told me that he had acquired a precious ticket for me to watch United play Newcastle at Wembley in the Charity Shield, the pre-season fixture between the league champions and the cup winners. (United had won both, so Newcastle were invited as league runners-up.) We sat among the Manchester United fans who chanted abuse throughout and who refused to sit down, because they did not want to, which was more a comment on the general bloody mindedness of society than any peculiar rudeness of United supporters. They were revolting, but Allan did not notice. He had talked in the past about the United 'family' and I thought that he had been joking; but, watching him at Wembley, I realised that he had been serious.

Allan could have been born in Halifax, Wrexham, Southend or even Brighton. If he had, perhaps he would not have fallen in love with his local club since it is easier to become addicted to one of the most glamorous clubs in the country than to a team whose idea of glory is not to be relegated. But I suspect that he would have followed Halifax Town as loyally as he did United because he was a fan waiting for a club; there are hundreds of thousands of men – and women – like Allan who live through their local teams. It is illogical and expensive but these are the people who have sustained football through the decades. The more enlightened lower division clubs try to cultivate this loyalty but it is different in the Premier League; here clubs need to generate tens of millions every season to survive and fans like Allan are a nuisance because they do not buy programmes and food at matches or waste their money on replica kit from club megastores. Much better if seats are occupied by young men with hearty appetites who will become the fathers of the boys who will demand the latest strip, at a reasonable £49.99 plus VAT, and a television which is tuned to the club's pay-as-you-view station, so that every away game, training session and cliché-ridden interview with the manager can be watched.

Allan and Elsie are pensioners and qualify for a variety of reduced rates but still spend about £1,300 a year on United. A father and two sons would probably pay more than £3,000 a year, excluding subscriptions to television channels. Allan knows that the Manchester United of the third millennium is not the same club that he first watched in 1944, when they played Manchester City in one of the irregular wartime games, using any players who happened to be available. That club had its roots in the community and players lived amongst them, earning average wages and living average lives, distanced from the supporters only by the fact that they were young and talented enough to be allowed to play for United.

From boyhood, Allan's life was inextricably bound to United. If United won at the weekend then Mondays were anticipated eagerly; if they lost, he knew that colleagues at work would enjoy his anguish. Allan and Elsie brought up two daughters and a son. Allan became a senior civil servant. He played football. And he watched United. There were disasters such as the Munich air crash of 6 February 1958 which wiped out many of the team which might have become the best in the history of English football. There were great years, too, when Old Trafford was home to some of the most dazzling players in history, such as Denis Law and Bobby Charlton. There were bleak years, when the history of the Busby era overpowered successive managers. Then Alex Ferguson, a dour, single-minded Scot, arrived.

Allan always insisted that *real* fans are the people who travel from the West Country or the South Coast to pay homage to United. He is just a chap who happens to live in the city. But this is too modest. He is the classic fan: realistic but also extraordinarily protective. He will debate the merits of United players over the decades and agree that only one player from the team of the late 1990s – the Dutch centre back Japp Stam – would get into an all-time great United team. He agrees with George Best when he says that Beckham cannot tackle, head the ball, does not score many goals and is generally overrated. Allan thinks that Beckham is a useful crosser of the ball but prefers Andrei Kanchelskis, from the early 1990s, as the best-ever right-sided attacker. Roy Keane, United's belligerent captain, who earns £50,000 a week, is competitive but is not, in Allan's opinion, in the same class as Duncan Edwards, who died at Munich. And he laughs at the idea that the 2000 crop of United strikers – Andy Cole, Dwight Yorke and Teddy Sheringham – are as good as Charlton, Law or Best. Can you imagine anyone going to a game because Yorke is playing, he asks.

Then loyalty kicks in. Today's players are dedicated professionals. He does not resent the fact that they are paid more in a week than he lives on in a year. Football is a circus and without them there would be no show.

Many years ago he used to turn up for a match at Old Trafford and pay at the gate. Now you need a season ticket – £418 a year for league games and about £22 for other fixtures – and these are almost as valuable as winning lottery tickets. Does he think that United are cynical? What did he think of the club's decision to withdraw from the FA Cup in the 1999–2000 season to play in FIFA's ridiculous World Club Championship in Brazil, a competition invented to make money for FIFA and the world's super-clubs, and which United regarded as an opportunity to enhance their global image? Surely, I asked, this shows that the club does not respect its supporters, who would prefer a glorious FA Cup run to a few matches against assorted Mexicans, Brazilians and Australians? Ah, well, he says, you have to remember that a club like United has to sell itself to pay the bills.

Another friend was captivated as a boy. Mick Brown is an unlikely football fan; a journalist on a national newspaper colour magazine, he writes elegant articles on religion, music and the arts. He recently returned from India, where he has been researching a story on the escape of a Tibetan lama. He did not, however, forget his beloved Crystal Palace while he was away; after discussing the intricacies of Buddhism and China's policies in the region with exiled monks, he was able to follow Palace's games on satellite television in his hotel room. Like Allan Corkindale he discovered his team when he was a child, in circumstances which would be unthinkable at today's Premier League grounds, with their all-season ticket, sell-out crowds.

Mick, who will shortly be celebrating his fiftieth birthday, was born a few minutes walk from Palace's Selhurst Park. His father took him to his first match in 1960 when he was nine, a Fourth Division game against Gillingham which Palace won 3-0. In the 1960s and 1970s Palace climbed steadily towards the First

Division, often watched by crowds of 30–40,000. But then the hooligans came and he drifted away, pursued a career and had a family. But, wherever he was – in New Orleans researching an article on a legendary saxophonist or trekking around India in search of mystics – he always worried about Palace: would they win, would they be relegated, would they go bankrupt? Now, with his family grown up, he has again become a regular at Selhurst Park, though it is much changed from the ground he once knew. A chunk has been turned into a supermarket. Fifteen thousand, not 40,000, is considered a good turn-out. He has thrown away the rattle he once whirled around his head, which is fortunate since he would be arrested today for carrying an offensive weapon.

But Mick is back home. Life has gone full circle; he began here as a boy, excited and eager, believing that anything was possible, for himself and Palace. But life is generally about disappointment, just as football is about clubs like Palace not Manchester United. 'Of course Palace matter,' he told me. 'Our fortunes have ebbed and flowed along similar lines. It's almost metaphysical.'

Rick Gekoski, an American who became a Coventry City fan when he was lecturing at Warwick University in 1971, describes the essence of the football supporter in his book, *Staying Up*. Gekoski, who had been invited to study how the club operated in the 1997–8 season, makes many telling observations – for example, that a player is a mercenary who sees his club as a temporary employer, just as a fan who works in a factory sees his company – but is especially effective when he talks about the fans. Coventry City only exists, he says, through its fans because they are permanent; directors, managers and players come and go but the supporters live through the club and give it reality. One day, he says, Highfield Road, City's home, will probably be turned into a 'nasty housing complex' and a new ground, perhaps called the Microprocessor Pentium II Stadium, will be thrown up on cheap land on the outskirts of the city.

The only things that will stay the same are the name 'Coventry

City Football Club' and us, its supporters. We are the club, we provide the community and the meaning. We have common memories, aspirations and desires, like a tribe or a nation. It is no wonder that the game means so much to us, and that we can behave so foolishly. We no longer have real villages, churches or communities, and the idea of nation, except at times of war or during the World Cup, fails to move us. So supporting our team focuses a lot of otherwise unallocated feeling, centres and intensifies it. At football matches thousands of otherwise emotionally inarticulate supporters bellow out, 'We Love You City, We Do!' when, I suspect, they would never overtly express that much love to their children.

I watched my first match at the Goldstone Ground, Hove, in the early 1960s. Brighton were playing Port Vale and I remember how vast the crowd and the ground seemed, though there were probably only a few thousand people in a cramped, nondescript stadium. On television players were tiny black and white shapes but here they appeared in Technicolor. They thudded into each other with frightening, unexpected power, though had this match been televised it would have been derided as an untidy scrap. But I was hooked and became a regular at the Goldstone until my mid-teens. In those days Brighton boomed. Roared on by crowds of 20,000, sometimes 30,000, they seemed destined to become a giant in the English game, which was only right since the town was rich and cosmopolitan and Brighton was the only league club in Sussex, one of the country's most affluent counties.

I used to turn up at the turnstiles and pay a few shillings to stand with my chums on the open terraces flanking one side of the pitch, opposite the creaky old grandstand peopled by strange creatures in sheepskin jackets and ties. The yobs stood behind one of the goals, but there was never any trouble. There was a handful of police, who strolled around the ground chatting to spectators about the game.

Social histories of England describe how football evolved into the main recreation of the working class between the world wars. Bigger disposable incomes, more leisure time, improved transport and the growth of the mass media meant that clubs flourished. Football had begun in the public schools, when one game involving a ball fractured into two separate sports – soccer and rugby – and had been played and watched by the upper and middle classes. By the 1920s, it had been taken over by the masses. By today's standards, attendances were breathtaking; 150,000 packed into the newly built Wembley for the first FA Cup Final there, between West Ham and Bolton Wanderers, when Bolton won 2-0 after a policeman on a white horse cleared the pitch of spectators.

In the years after the Second World War, a grim period of low wages and rationing, football – and the football pools – offered an escape from the drudgery of real life. In 1948–9 more than 41 million people watched a total of 1,848 league matches, in Divisions One, Two and Three (North and South). More games were played in the 1950s but the number of people watching them fell inexorably for a variety of social and economic reasons, none of which had anything to do with the appallingly primitive facilities offered to spectators. By the 1972–3 season, fewer than 25 million were watching football. By then hooliganism was beginning to drive peaceful, law-abiding fans away. In 1982–3 the figure was 19 million; in 1985–6 it was less than 16 million, which meant that football had lost 24 million customers in four decades.

The First Division suffered the greatest numerical loss, which was inevitable since the crowds here had been the largest in the late 1940s. In 1985–6, 9 million watched games in the top division, compared with almost 18 million in the late forties. The decline was even more dramatic in the Second Division: 3.5 million in 1985–6, compared with more than 11 million in the late 1940s. Since most of the violence occurred in the First Division (though every club had its gang of dedicated troublemakers) there were other factors behind the decline, such as the fact that the average bloke had better things to do on Saturday afternoons than get cold and wet in a crumbling stadium.

The Fans

The fall was sharp, too, in percentage terms, in the lower divisions. The Second Division drew more than 11.5 million fans in the late 1940s and just over 3.5 million in the mid-1980s, which was pathetic; the Third Division North and South had once attracted almost 12 million but by the 1980s the Third and Fourth Divisions could not even muster 4 million. These small clubs, which had once been the focal point of a community, looked doomed; the new generation of fans, reared on top-class televised matches, could not be bothered with crude, scruffy games, while the older supporters, whose lives had once been entwined with their clubs, were dying.

Then came salvation: the World Cup in Italy in 1990, the Taylor Report of 1991 and the new Premier League in 1992. Suddenly the game became glamorous and fashionable as satellite television poured hundreds of millions into it. Stadia were more comfortable. The hooligans did not disappear but they were corralled more effectively by the police, using a combination of electronic surveillance and intelligence.

By the late 1990s, almost 11 million people were watching the Premier League every season, a rise of 3 million since the dark days of the late 1980s. In Division One, formerly Division Two, there was also a revival, from 4 million to over 8 million. But ominously for the smaller clubs there was little improvement in Divisions Two and Three, which suggested that modern fans wanted the best or nothing.

Statistics can prove anything, and it could be argued that these conclusions are misleading because they ignore such factors as the decreased capacities of stadia in the safety-conscious 1990s. But it would be hard to dispute the basic point: football is *generally* not as popular as it once was and those people who actually go to games, as opposed to watching on television, are more interested in the Arsenals and Manchester Uniteds – even if this means long journeys – than their local teams.

Shortly after the new season began in 1999 it seemed that football would implode from greed and overexposure. There were

27

only fragments of evidence to support this theory – disappointing crowds at certain matches; a supporter who gave up her season ticket and subscription to satellite television in protest against rising prices; a row over the cost of football boots endorsed by David Beckham – but many commentators argued that the revolt would grow, as more people realised that they were being ripped off so that ordinary players could earn upwards of £30,000 a week.

Some statistics supported this theory. Wages in the Premiership had more than tripled in five seasons and had shot up by an astonishing 40 per cent in one year. Clubs now paid the four hundred or so players in the top division almost £200 million a year, an average of £500,000 per player.

Although television finances much of this, the fans are also being asked to pay more, and evidence suggests that they are beginning to realise that they are being ripped off. Thus, attendances are slipping. Aston Villa's fell by 22.92 per cent in the first months of the 1999–2000 season, Derby's by 12.66 per cent and Wimbledon's by almost 20 per cent. In the Football League there were similar drops: 30 per cent of Stoke's support vanished; Bournemouth mislaid over 30 per cent of its fans; and Rotherham 26.10 per cent.

Prices are the key factor. Alison Pilling, the chairwoman of the Football Supporters' Association, gave up her season ticket at Leeds United and cancelled her subscription to BSkyB, which had cost £27 a month. 'My bank manager told me that I had been overdrawn once too often. I still try to go to games but the cheapest ticket I could get for one (against Liverpool) was £23. I have two young sons who like to go and when prices were reasonable it didn't matter if they were bored by half-time. It's become a game for people with money and has lost a lot of goodwill of real fans. If the gates fall and clubs suddenly open their doors to the traditional supporters they have pushed away they will take a lot of persuading to come back.'

Even more critical was Mark Longden of the Independent Manchester United Supporters' Association, whose members fear that United only cares about money. 'The Premier League is being swallowed up by a commercial tidal wave. I believe that the game will self-destruct within five years,' he said bluntly.

Some small clubs, however, reported rises in attendances between 1997 and 1998, and 1998 and 1999. Colchester United in Division Two recorded an increase of 44.2 per cent, but that, alas, meant only that average crowds were 4,479 instead of 3,137, which might have been enough for a part-time outfit but was nowhere near big enough to sustain a league side. There were also superficially impressive percentage rises in the Third Division: Hull City up by almost 30 per cent; Carlisle by 38 per cent; and Swansea by an amazing 51.8 per cent. Translated into actual people, however, these figures are tiny: Swansea, for example, averaged 5,225 people per game. Even Brighton shot up by almost 40 per cent; unfortunately that meant an average crowd of just over 3,000 compared with the previous season's lamentable 2,329. It does not require a degree in business administration to realise that crowds like these cannot support a league club.

Everything is about money today. Since football is big business, City analysts now track its profits and losses and the figures are more alarming every year. For the 1996–7 season, the wage bill in the Premiership was £361 million, up by 25 per cent on the previous season. Only two players had earned £1 million in 1996–7 but a year later *seventy* players, the majority of them uncapped, anonymous journeymen, picked up £1 million for a season's work.

Poor Brighton show how clubs can reach the heights and then plummet, trapped by players on wages which the club cannot afford. Failure means fewer supporters, less money and relegation, which in turn further reduces crowds. The Goldstone, Brighton's home for almost a century, was sold secretly by the club's owners on the eve of the 1995–6 season. The few thousand fans who had remained loyal complained that the club had been stripped by its cynical owners; they protested loudly, invaded the pitch and generally embarrassed the football authorities, who did not appreciate the way that these people were drawing attention to the fact that small clubs like Albion were perceived as cash cows by businessmen and then left to die. The fans won a partial victory – the FA devised a survival plan which ensured the club's future as an independent entity, with its own ground – but the harsh reality was that, without a generous benefactor such as Blackburn's Jack Walker, who spent more than £60 million in the 1990s trying to turn the club into a giant, it was hard to see how Albion would ever amass the money to pay for a new stadium and, more important, the players who would lift the club back into the big time.

For two seasons, while Albion tried to find a new base, and a reason to continue to exist, they played 'home' games at Gillingham in faraway Kent. After two dreadful years there they persuaded Brighton and Hove Council, which still viewed football as an unwelcome C and D activity, rather than a sport which would generate tens of millions for the town, to lease an athletics stadium in Brighton while they raised the money for a proper home. Fans throughout the country could not believe that this had happened. As I read the stories about Albion playing on a pitch in a stadium which hosted the Sussex U14s athletics finals when I was a boy, I recalled how I had watched them at Wembley in the FA Cup Final in 1983 against Manchester United. Albion would have won that day if Gordon Smith had not contrived to miss from a few inches in the last minute; United pulverised Albion in the replay.

Amidst this gloom there were heartening stories about the resurrection of clubs which had been bankrupt. But these rescues came courtesy of that traditional figure, the local businessman made good, not the initiatives of fans. Third Division Darlington were doomed until George Reynolds, an ex-safe-breaker-turned-multimillionaire manufacturer of cut-price kitchen worktops, flourished his cheque book, cleared the club's £5.5 million debt and bought new players. He paid for a new 25,000 all-seater stadium fit for the new century and, because he felt guilty about being so rich (*The Sunday Times* ranked him as the eighty-seventh richest person in the country, with £240 million in the bank) slashed season ticket prices so that the less well off could follow the team.

Fulham, once of the First Division, had enjoyed the services of Johnny Haynes, the first £100-a-week footballer in the early 1960s. The club had been about style and humour; in the mid-1970s they had become a kind of all-stars veterans XI, as Bobby Moore and George Best played out the final days of momentous careers. Their ground, Craven Cottage, overlooking the Thames, is homely, eccentric and mischievous but it is also prime real estate in one of the most fashionable parts of London.

The fans had resisted the efforts of developers over the years to turn Craven Cottage into luxury flats but they could not give the club what it needed to survive: money. Then, in May 1997, Mohammed al Fayed bought Fulham. Al Fayed is the fascinating, ridiculous owner of Harrods and father of Dodi, who died with Diana, Princess of Wales, in a car crash in Paris. He thought that MPs could be bought, he sued, and was sued, frequently and he complained loudly about the injustice of not being given a British passport. But whatever you think of him, and many do not think much, no one can dispute that he transformed Fulham. In the 1998–9 season the club's average attendance was 11,387, up from 9,018 the previous season. This income did not pay the wages of the manager, Kevin Keegan, who later left to lead England, or the purchase of Premier League-class players; al Fayed's wallet did that.

In the 1980s I spent a week at Halifax Town, researching a story for *The Sunday Times*. It was a curiously moving experience; Halifax had no right to be in the Football League since its ground was a decrepit dog track. Its players were either has-beens from the lower divisions or young men who had once been on the books of major clubs and who still wore their old club blazers, as if they were trying to convince the public, and themselves, that they did not belong there. The team was hopeless; I watched them practise a variation on West Ham's corner to the near post but the players could not hit the ball anywhere near the vital spot.

The dressing rooms were carpeted with artificial turf, cadged from a local firm. The pitch was maintained by an old man with a lawnmower. The stadium consisted of a creaky stand, terracing and a grass bank behind one goal. But Halifax would not give up. They organised an open day for the faithful; it was sad to see the players, in their team blazers, waiting for the thousands who never came. A few hundred people, mostly children, turned up.

A few years later I went to Torquay, which had ousted Halifax as the worst side in the league, and it was the same story: effort and hope in defiance of reality. The stadium was smarter, though not by much, but the team was the same blend of optimistic youth and disillusioned older players, who had slid down the league as their legs lost power. Match day was a few thousand people, who laughed and jeered at the team's discomfort as they lost yet again.

Once it was easy to describe the type of people who went to football matches. Most of the fans who stood on the terraces were working-class men. Fathers brought their sons, just as they had been brought by their fathers. In the cheaper seats were the foremen, the lower middle classes and a few women. The best seats were occupied by the local toffs, often accompanied by their wives.

Conditions for the majority were awful. Fans were often packed so tightly on the terraces that they had to urinate where they stood because it was impossible to move. Apart from occasional ill-tempered scuffles, violence was unknown. By the late 1960s, however, the old industrial working class was disintegrating. The family and religion, the cement of society, were irrelevant. Young men sought a new identity on the terraces. They organised gangs and waged war on opposing fans. This was not mindless violence, as the tabloids alleged, but an attempt to find purpose and identity.

The Sir Norman Chester Centre for Football Research at Leicester University analysed the people in the mid-1990s who followed Premier League teams. The survey told us nothing that we did not know already and, as the centre admitted, was so small – based on just over 15,000 people – that it was impossible to draw definitive conclusions from it. The centre's researchers complained that many clubs had not bothered to forward questionnaires to fans. They also said that answering questions in writing was an activity for older A / Bs and so they did not discover much about young, poor males, who are vital for the survival of football.

But, despite these limitations, trends emerged. Parents were more willing to take children to games because grounds were 'safer'. Season ticket holders were drawn from all social classes, many were born near the club they supported, and many did not care about the national team. New fans and subscribers to BSkyB liked the Premier League. It is obvious to anyone that Premier League crowds now contain more middle-class people and more women and children than in the grim days of the mid-1980s. Many of the fans who stroll past my friend Gillian's house in Chelsea en route to post-match tapas look to me as if they have just been to the opera, but the majority of supporters at Stamford Bridge remain working-class males, for whom football is an opportunity to drink, swear and bond with their mates.

In 2000 another survey revealed that a third of the new fans in the Premiership were women, which meant that one in seven of those watching games here were women, an increase of 16 per cent since 1997. This was proof, said Richard Scudamore, chief executive of the Premier League, that players were 'like pop or film stars'. The new Premiership fan spent around £320 on a season ticket and another £94 a year on 'merchandising', was losing interest in traditional local derbies and enjoyed watching big European games on television. The more affluent fans are not as interested in the lower divisions. Here the crowd – if that is the word to describe a huddle of 2,000 people – is a traditional mix of solid older fans, from all social groups, and young males, for whom their team, however useless, represents excitement.

The hooligans of the 1970s and 1980s have not vanished. They may be less visible today but there are still gangs at every club whose idea of a fun Saturday is to launch an assault on a rival 'firm'. There have been excellent books and documentaries about these thugs and we now know that the view of the stereotype thug – a thick, scruffy drunkard – is hopelessly naive. There are hooligans like this but many are intelligent and in their twenties or thirties, or even older. Many are married, with mortgages, children and good jobs. They are hooligans – shorthand for a fan who likes fighting – because it is fun; they organise 'rucks' by mobile phone, delight in trying to outwit the police and see football as a way of making their lives more dramatic. In summary, they demonstrate that many people are instinctively violent and unpleasant, and clubs and football administrators cannot change that.

A new creature has also emerged: the 'celebrity' fan. Politicians, actors and actresses, novelists, disc jockeys, models and anyone else whose livelihood depends on popularity have suddenly announced that they love football.

When they are short on ideas, newspapers and magazines ask celebrities to describe their obsession with, say, Leyton Orient, Bury or Burnley. Sometimes these interviewees are genuine. One magazine spoke to five well-known people who were obviously telling the truth; this might not have been riveting journalism but at least it was honest.

Chris Eubank, the former champion middleweight boxer, announced that, though he lives in Brighton, he supports Spurs (match tickets from £28; season tickets from £560). He did not claim infatuation from childhood, but, with his usual modesty, said that he became interested in the club after two players, Gary Lineker and Paul Gascoigne, came to watch him fight.

The actor Phil Moriarty said that he had switched from Millwall – because he did not think that the club was doing enough to attract young supporters – to Wimbledon (match tickets from £25; season tickets from £220) because they had always been underdogs. He did not pretend that he was an ordinary fan; he wears a suit and likes to relax in the players' lounge, a facility not available to most supporters.

Another actor, Ray Winstone, has followed West Ham (match tickets from £25; season tickets from £435) since he was a boy.

Here was the voice of the old-fashioned fan; he worshipped the late, great Bobby Moore, drinks in pubs outside the ground after the game, wants West Ham to play local or at least English players and hates multinational teams like Chelsea.

The actress Charlie Moloney had been watching Chelsea (match tickets from £25; season tickets from £410) and the pop singer Leeroy of Prodigy was mad about Arsenal (match tickets from £25; season tickets from £220). And, like most fans, he detests Manchester United.

But it is difficult to be sure about the sincerity of many other celebrity fans. Amongst the hundreds of sites on the Internet dedicated to football one lists the famous – and those who would like to be famous – and their clubs.

Predictably, the glamour clubs, such as Arsenal and Liverpool, are 'supported' by dozens of celebrities but the minnows also have their famous fans. For example, a TV presenter, whom I had never heard of, apparently adores Bournemouth, a television weatherman likes Burnley, an actress follows Swansea and a film director is crazy about Portsmouth. No doubt all these people are genuine but, as I scroll down the list, it occurs to me that football was not so popular amongst celebrities when the sport was broke and unfashionable.

It would be simplistic to say that clubs despise their fans but fair to say that they believe that fans will always be there; that they will always pay more and that they will remain loyal, no matter how many foreign mercenaries are signed. There have been attempts to curb price rises – notably by the Government's Football Task Force, set up in 1997 to probe the sport and led by ex-MP David Mellor, best remembered because an affair with an 'actress' wrecked his political career – but football has always rebuffed them. The reality is that prices keep rising because clubs need the money to pay players. Clubs extend stadia because larger crowds mean more money but, in turn, ticket prices have to go up to finance building work.

Manchester United represent the best, and the worst, of the football club as a business. United, the publicly listed company, regards the people who actually go to Old Trafford as the tip of the consumer iceberg; the 60,000 souls who regularly turn up to watch matches at Old Trafford spend millions of pounds every season on tickets, programmes and food and in shops in the ground, but there are millions more in Britain and abroad who support the team. United is also a great football club and so there is a lingering, sentimental attachment to the past, when fans and players travelled to games on the same buses and drank afterwards in the same pubs.

United introduced a membership scheme in the 1987–8 season in an attempt to boost revenue. The club already had 20,000 season ticket holders and thought that it might be able to attract a similar number to the new scheme, in return for what Barry Moorhouse, the official responsible for the project, called 'a package of benefits, such as discounts at the souvenir shops'. By the mid-1990s there were 40,000 season ticket holders and another 140,000 'members' competing for the 20,000 or so remaining seat at Old Trafford. Moorhouse said that the days of paying at the turnstiles were long gone. Thus, success had created a new problem. Only people with tickets could see United, which meant that crowds were ageing. But the club were marketing hard, through television and the Internet, and hoped to attract young supporters in this way, even though most would never actually see the team in the flesh.

This is the new world of most United fans: he or she has a virtual reality relationship with the club, and the 60,000 who are lucky enough to be at Old Trafford are there to provide the atmosphere for the millions watching on their computers, televisions and mobile phones. Clubs still insist that the fans in the ground matter – Everton reckoned in 1999 that £9 million of its annual turnover of £19 million came from gate receipts – and say that the new wealthy fans will subsidise traditional supporters. Clubs might want to believe this but the fact is that Premiership grounds are no-go areas for the young and less well off. This will not matter if the new fans remain loyal but it will be disastrous if they decide that football is, after all, just twenty-two blokes kicking a ball.

Fans know that they are being exploited. During the 1997–8 season, the total income generated by the professional game in England was £829 million, a rise of 23 per cent on the previous season. Meanwhile, players' salaries rose by an average 29 per cent in the four divisions. But these figures disguised the growing gulf between the Premier League and the rest; the Premier League clubs posted pre-tax profits for the first time since 1995 but the other seventy-two clubs announced that they had lost a total of almost £53 million, the worst ever result.

Premier League clubs turned over £570 million, and paid £294 million in wages, an increase of 25 per cent in the year. In the First Division clubs turned over £175 million and paid wages of £118 million; in the Second Division the figures were £66 million and £55 million; and in the Third, £27 million and £26 million. From this it is clear that clubs in the top division are managing to pay players' huge salaries – though many are finding it hard – but in the lower divisions income barely covers salaries.

The top clubs can increase prices and demand more from television. Chelsea once increased season ticket prices by 47 per cent in the knowledge that there were enough people with the money to pay. It did not matter that this policy would drive away the young and less well off, who were the traditional supporters. Other clubs are more cautious but prices have risen by four times the rate of inflation since the Premier League was formed. Chelsea's wage bill rose by an astonishing 81 per cent in a year, which the club could afford; but other clubs, desperate to remain in the league, tried to keep pace. Derby's wage bill rose by 79 per cent.

The saga of replica kits illustrates how many clubs regard their fans. It was estimated that sales of these horrible nylon outfits were worth £200 million a year to clubs in the Premier and Football League in the late 1990s.

The first club to notice a fall in sales was Newcastle United, after two directors, Douglas Hall and Freddy Shepherd, told an undercover reporter from the *News of the World* that Newcastle fans were daft for paying £40 for replica shirts which cost only £5 to manufacture. This was their least offensive comment; they also bragged about their sexual conquests, denounced United's players and described Geordie women as 'dogs'. Following the exposé, it was reported that sales of the club's 'branded products' had dropped from £5.5 million over six months to £3.3 million. Newcastle denied that this had anything to do with the outburst by Messrs Hall and Shepherd. They claimed that fans had been put off shopping in the club store because the stadium was being expanded and people did not like shopping in a building site. The club's spokesman mumbled about the 'general retail environment', even citing the difficulties that Marks and Spencer were experiencing. But he did not address the interesting question: had fans finally realised that replica kits were ugly and overpriced?

Adults who buy this replica junk have only themselves to blame but parents are under constant pressure from their children, who want to wear the same kit as their heroes. The clubs know this and change strips regularly, which means that parents either have to tell little Johnny or Sarah that they have to wear an out-of-date shirt, which would not be good for domestic relations, or find £40 for the new model.

Since football supporters are also voters, politicians have warned the clubs that they are exploiting their fans, but the clubs take no notice. Manchester United, for example, have changed their away strip *thirteen* times in five years. Fulham change their away strip every year. The *Guardian* alerted its readers to what was happening; it warned readers that Fulham expected fans to spend £67.97, the cost of a shirt, shorts and socks, on new home and away outfits.

The fans have begun to revolt. Manchester United have revealed that shirt sales fell by 20 per cent in a year, and Spurs reported that income from shirt sales fell by 11 per cent. Leeds United also suffered. The sales teams running these multimillion pound operations decided that they needed better quality 'leisure wear'. So the megastores attached to stadia now resemble department stores, with club and sponsors' logos on clothes where designer labels are usually found. At Chelsea, one of the most efficiently commercial clubs in the country, the shop looks like a boutique on the King's Road. The club calculates, rightly, that fans prefer to buy clothes here rather than in ordinary shops; the fact that this 'loyalty' is required because Chelsea's players earn more in a week than the average fan makes in a year is not considered revelant.

It would be foolish to romanticise the days when fans were grateful to be herded onto terraces to watch players who were treated like serfs by their clubs. Sport is now a multibillion pound industry which is part of the new global economy of high-tech entertainment and leisure. But a football stadium is *not* a private health club. A club depends on ordinary men and women whose lives are inextricably tied to it, not the new fans who drive to grounds in company cars and who watch games quietly, while they chat about house prices and school fees. Eventually, when these fans realise that football cannot become more exciting, they will find new ways to spend their money. A football club needs to be sustained by rowdiness, grit and passion, but these are not qualities welcome in the Premiership and amongst the aspiring giants of the First Division. These clubs must find a way to merge tradition and innovation; they must acknowledge that the young and the poor, who are scruffy and noisy fans and who are not interested in, or cannot afford, half-time feasts of yoghurt and goat's cheese baguettes, are as important as the season ticket holders who think that a £10 match programme is a bargain. If the clubs will not act, the fans should; they should boycott matches, shun megastores and Internet sites selling junk replica kit until clubs realise that, without them, football will cease to exist. But fans are probably too loyal to inflict such punishment.

The football authorities, clubs and supporters' pressure groups exchange plans for salary caps, for distributing money from television more fairly and for setting aside more seats for the young and those on low incomes, but the truth is that the society which created football has vanished and the free market is defining the sport. But admitting that a problem is complex does not mean that it is insoluble. Football knows that it faces a long-term crisis. However, it has always been greedy; today is good and tomorrow will be better, so no one cares what will happen in ten years.

The old fans will never let go. In March 2000, after newspapers ran front page stories about David Beckham's new hair style – he had shaved his head to prove that he was as tough and committed as Roy Keane, United's captain – I told Allan Corkindale that it was ridiculous that Beckham, who was after all not that special, should attract so much attention. He joked back that Beckham had spoilt the hard man effect with an earring, but I sensed that he was not comfortable with the direction of the conversation. I could not resist. Surely, I asked, it was time to protest about the grotesque commercialisation of his team by giving up his season tickets. He laughed, as if I had gone completely mad. Meanwhile, Mick Brown was slaving over yet another erudite article for his magazine. But he was distracted. Crystal Palace's financial problems were so grave that the club might fold. It was impossible to imagine life without Palace. What could be done, Mick asked me, genuinely and deeply distressed.

The new fans are not like this; for them football is a lifestyle statement, like owning a home with the right postcode, driving the latest BMW and eating sushi. But times change and one day football will become unfashionable again and they will drift away, agreeing with each other that, actually, they don't see the point of the game.

Chapter Three

The Hornby Effect

In 1992 Nick Hornby, a thirty-five-year-old former teacher who had become a freelance journalist, published *Fever Pitch*, a book which chronicles his lifelong obsession with Arsenal. It became a bestseller and made Hornby rich and famous. His next books, *High Fidelity* and *About a Boy*, showed that it had not been a fluke. But no matter how many splendid books he writes, Hornby will be remembered forever as the author of the style bible of the new football, as it changed from a sport practised by morons and watched by cretins to become *the* subject of the 1990s – fashionable, arty, glitzy and significant.

This is ironic because *Fever Pitch* celebrates the old football, not the sport of all-seater stadia, executive boxes and overpriced players who appear on the covers of colour magazines with young women draped around them. The book is the voice of the boy whose life becomes inextricably linked to a club. For Hornby it was Arsenal, though he grew up in a dull satellite town outside London – and, briefly, when he was at university, Cambridge United – but it could have been Liverpool, Newcastle, Wolverhampton Wanderers, Bury, Halifax or even Brighton and Hove Albion.

Hornby rejoiced in the glorious squalor of Highbury, Arsenal's grand old stadium in north London. He was not interested in comfortable seats with good views of the pitch; he always stood behind a goal, jammed in, straining to watch the action, screaming encouragement and abuse. He did not support Arsenal because they were successful – they were not when he first saw them; nor because they were exciting – even when they scooped trophies they were one of the most boring teams in the country. He followed Arsenal because fate had decreed that he should, which is how people become tied to clubs. Hornby's football reflected life, a series of disappointments punctuated by fleeting, unexpected triumphs. He never had any faith in Arsenal, or in life, which meant that their successes were sweet.

Until *Fever Pitch*, the literature of football had been poetic, investigative or grimly descriptive. Novelists wrote elegantly, as if football were the theatre or New Wave cinema, journalists probed scandals and reformed hooligans dictated semi-literate memoirs about the thrill of slashing rivals with broken bottles. But Hornby explained how it was possible for an otherwise sane, peace-loving man like him to live through a football team. His description of decades on the terraces at Highbury was also an examination of middle-class urban man, an angst-ridden creature who sought refuge in football because real life – failed relationships, stalled careers and diminishing physical powers – was so confusing. Hornby was north London's answer to American television programmes like *Seinfeld*, *Frasier*, *The Larry Sanders Show* and *Friends*, where truths about love, vanity, ambition and friendship are punched home in one-line gags wrapped inside plots where nothing happens.

I bought *Fever Pitch* in paperback reluctantly. I had avoided it in hardback because I could not bear to read the work of a fraud who had appropriated my obsession to turn himself into a celebrity millionaire. I recalled asking a publisher a few years earlier whether he would be interested in my memoir of life as a Brighton fan and failed player and he had sniffed; surely you realise, he said, that books about football don't sell?

I started with the reviews, arranged at the front of *Fever Pitch*. It was galling. 'A smart and wonderful book' (*New Statesman*). '. . . the first book that gives a credible explanation of why

someone becomes a supporter' (*The Times Saturday Review*).
'. . . he makes the terrace life seem not just plausible but sometimes
near heroic in its single-minded vehemence, its heart-shaking highs
and lows' (*Independent on Sunday*). 'He has put his finger on
truths that have been unspoken for generations' (*Irish Times*).
'Utterly hilarious. Even football-haters will be beguiled' (*Elle*).
The fact that *Elle* was enthusiastic summed up the new football.

I wanted to hate the book but could not put it down; it was
incomparably better than anything that I could have written.
Having accepted that Hornby was soccer writing's Pele and that I
was the equivalent of a park footballer I could enjoy his book.
Unlike the film of *Fever Pitch*, a trite love story about two teachers,
there were many strands in the book. There was witty reportage,
charting games played by Arsenal (and occasionally Cambridge)
from the late 1960s until the early 1990s. There were astute
observations on fans, players and managers and the differences
between major clubs and the nonentities of the lower leagues.
Hornby was compelling on football as a reflection of society; the
sport had been built on a nation of factories and mines and had
almost died, along with the old industries, before emerging into a
present of mobile phones, of short-term contracts, City bonuses and
multi-channel television. Cementing all this was Hornby, demanding to know of himself why Arsenal mattered so much.

Fever Pitch showed that football is a predator, which creeps up
on young boys and captures them; one day you are a normal kid
and the next you are possessed. Hornby's life was changed in the
autumn of 1968 when his father took him to Highbury to watch
Arsenal play Stoke City in the First Division. The details of that
afternoon – the smell of cigarettes and pies, the faces, contorted
with the happy fury of fans who are absorbed by the awfulness of
their team and the primitive power of it all – remained with Hornby
for the rest of his life. My first visit to the Goldstone Ground, home
of Brighton and Hove Albion, overlooking the detached houses and
neat open spaces of Hove Park, was not as vivid; it was the early
1960s and they were playing Port Vale in the Third Division. I

cannot remember who took me there – it was certainly not my father, a gentle man who was always so tired from his work as a salesman in a department store that he slept on Saturday afternoons – but I recall standing by the wall bordering the pitch and being thrilled. Compared to Highbury and the First Division, the Goldstone and Port Vale was nothing, but football seduces in many guises; to a small boy this was magic.

The Rothman's Football Yearbook, the encyclopaedia of the game, covers Brighton in the 1960s with a few terse facts about largest crowds and biggest wins but I remember the Goldstone filling every Saturday with 30,000 people to enjoy the Albion scoring four, five or six goals against Fourth and then Third Division teams. There are dozens of clubs like Brighton, which are just names on pools coupons except to those poor souls who are hopelessly addicted to them. A few teams, like Brighton in the early 1980s, rose briefly to national prominence by getting into the top division or by reaching an FA Cup Final before sinking back to their rightful place in the lower orders. But for most fans football consists of their own teams, who toil while another sport, played by Liverpool, Arsenal, Manchester United, Chelsea and the rest, happens on television.

But, perhaps because Brighton were not Arsenal, where the dramas were so much more powerful, the team did not take over my life. When Brighton were at home I would run the mile or so from our rented flat near the seafront in Hove and join pals from school on the open terraces. We never went behind the goals, because the view was bad and because we were nice grammar school boys and did not want to join the louts from the secondary modern who chanted like madmen. I used to pop up to the ground during the holidays to watch the players crash around the concrete five-a-side pitch beneath the grandstand which doubled up as a staff car park; they always signed autographs as they made their way after training to the café opposite, to tuck into fish and chips and study the racing papers.

I still recall some of the players. There was tiny Brian Powney in goal, who had springs for legs. We had Norman Gall, an elegant centre half who was once tipped to join Spurs, and muscular Dave Turner at left half, who was indestructible. At right half there was a young Welshman called Barrie Rees who seemed destined for greatness until he was killed in a car crash. I remember reading the front page report of his death in the *Evening Argus* and thinking that life was unfair and cruel – which shows that football can be instructive.

Then we bought Bobby Smith from Spurs, a stocky centre forward from the Double-winning side of 1960–1 who had played fifteen times for England and scored thirteen goals. When Smith made his debut against Barrow, 35,000 packed the Goldstone; I can still see him rise on the penalty spot and flick a header into the top corner. But Smith had come to Albion because he was finished, not because the club was going anywhere. A few months later I went to a reserve game and saw him, so fat that he could hardly walk, let alone run, topple over when he tried to kick the ball.

I relished our games at lunchtime on the playing fields at the front of the school, where there were two, full-size pitches for the older boys, and two smaller ones for the youngsters. We threw down jackets for goalposts and selected our teams; a few minutes after the school had emptied the entire field was a mass of running, tackling and shouting boys, acting out the fantasy that they were Bobby Charlton or Jimmy Greaves.

We played constantly in proper games against rival houses (grammar schools were modelled on public schools) and other schools. There were school teams for every age group, under 12s, under 13s, up to the Second and the First Team. We had real strips, with numbers on the shirts, and travelled to away games on Saturday mornings on coaches, just like professionals. Other schools had even better pitches than us; the public schools had manicured grounds which were as good as today's Premier League surfaces.

Football was the Albion at the Goldstone Ground, and playing at school, at parks and at recreation grounds around Hove. It was only on television as a treat. On Saturday nights, providing that my Mum and Dad did not want to watch a Frank Sinatra special, I could watch BBC's *Match of the Day*, and marvel at Denis Law and George Best. On Sunday afternoons Southern Television had highlights from a local match. Often it was Southampton, starring an England international called Terry Paine, who was clumsy and ugly, or Portsmouth, whom I hated so much, for no good reason, that I preferred to spend my time kicking a ball against the beach huts than watch them. In May there was the Cup Final. Broadcasting began at lunchtime, with reviews of the teams' progress to the Final, interviews with the players at their hotels and with fans as they descended on Wembley, and studio discussions about the forthcoming game, in which a pompous chap called Jimmy Hill, wearing a remarkable chin and beard, always spoke well. I stocked up for these special days with crisps, chocolate and soft drinks.

Most unforgettable of all was the afternoon of 30 July 1966 at Wembley when England beat West Germany 4-2, after extra time, and won the World Cup. I remember jumping up and down on the sofa as Kenneth Wolstenholme, the voice of football, uttered the immortal words, which spawned a successful chat show in the late 1990s, as Geoff Hurst thundered towards the German goal. 'They think it's all over,' Wolstenholme shouted as fans prematurely invaded the pitch. There was an instant of silence. Then he added, with genius: 'It is now.'

Occasionally, I saw the legends of Wolstenholme's world in the flesh. Once, Chelsea visited the Goldstone for an FA Cup tie. They had Peter Bonetti, aka 'the Cat', in goal; Ron 'Chopper' Harris, a small half back built of solid muscle whom I had often seen scything down opponents on television; and Peter Osgood, a tall, languid centre forward. I can still hear the crunch as Harris and my hero, Dave Turner, smashed into each other and flew into the perimeter wall. Both men got up, smiled and strode off. Today, they would have feigned dreadful injury, spat at each other and been sent off. Television would have analysed the incident in slow motion from a dozen cameras, revealing that Harris's spittle had not actually hit Turner, and newspapers would have condemned the whole affair. But these were two hard men doing an honest job for a fair wage; they were not egomaniacal, spoilt millionaires.

When I was almost fourteen I was selected for the town team, Brighton Boys. It was an immense honour and I was puffed up with pride. Looking back today I realise that I only got there by effort. I was small and fast but was more effective in park games than on full-sized pitches. Once I played at the Goldstone Ground, against Hastings Boys, and remember my stomach churning when the schoolmaster, who was our manager, told me that I would be playing at centre half. I spent the game digging holes in the centre circle with my studs while our centre forward smashed in six goals.

The realisation that I was getting worse rather than better with age was confirmed the following season when I was a member of the Brighton and Hove Albion youth team. Again, this is not as impressive as it seemed at the time to me, or my friends. A few dozen lads had attended a selection session at the Goldstone. Most were hopeless and were rejected, leaving me and twenty others, most of whom came from secondary moderns and would become bricklayers or plumbers or petty criminals if they did not make the grade as professional footballers. In those days even First Division footballers were within reach; a handful, like George Best, were more pop stars than athletes but the rest were simply doing all right. Players for teams like Brighton were only earning a living, like my Dad.

I knew that I was not good enough to be a professional, but did not care. Being a professional for a club like Albion was not an appealing prospect; the money was bad and the career was short. One of my heroes in the 1st XI at school had been signed by Leyton Orient but had never made it to the First Division; like so many others, he was a journeyman, hacking out a living at Darlington, Halifax and Exeter. I dreamt of travelling to exotic places, of university and being successful in some other, as yet unspecified, manner. But the other lads in the Albion youth team needed this; if they failed, adult life would be lugging bricks and fitting central heating systems.

We trained hard and I became gloriously fit. I remember running for a bus to get to school. I caught it effortlessly, as if propelled by a jet engine, thanks to the Albion. But I never made the youth team. The other players were hungrier and better and I drifted away. None, however, was offered apprenticeships and I never heard of any of them again.

The fitness stayed for a few weeks. I played for the school second team against the 1st XI. I ran and ran and ran and could have gone on for ever. But it did not last. In my next game I was tired after twenty minutes.

There are moments which seem trivial at the time but which, in retrospect, define our lives. We miss an opportunity at work, which shapes our career because the chance never comes again. We have a row with a girlfriend and break up and realise, many years later, that she was the one. We trust a friend with a confidence and are betrayed. One such moment came when I was playing in a seven-a-side tournament for the school at Brighton Grammar. I tackled a player and saw my ankle swivel, as if it was made of rubber. The pain was excruciating.

I hobbled off the pitch and sat down. This was the era when physiotherapists were old fellows with sponges who sprinted on to the pitch on *Match of the Day*. Schoolboys who were injured went to their GPs and were given a bandage and an aspirin. So I went home on the bus, put some ice on the ankle and thought that I would be playing next day. But the pain became so unbearable that I was forced to go to Casualty at Hove General. There the ankle was X-rayed, pronounced unbroken and wrapped in a bandage. Next day after school I changed for second team training but the ankle felt weak and sore. I tried to run and it hurt. When I tried to kick the ball a hot poker went through me. Perhaps I would have given up football anyway. I was almost sixteen and was bored with the Albion. My friends had grown their hair and spent their Saturdays listening to music and puffing silly cigarettes containing particles of illegal substances. I had passed my O' Levels and was determined now to do well at my A' Levels and, who knows, perhaps have a crack at getting into Oxford. I wanted to travel, too, and that summer bought a ferry ticket to France, from where I hitched to Spain. Back at school, insulated from punishment because I was a candidate for the Oxbridge entrance examinations, I set about causing as much trouble as possible; I formed a school 'council' to negotiate with the authorities on such weighty matters as hair length and told the PE master that football was history.

But the ankle still throbbed. Then someone told me about a physiotherapist in a place called Balham, somewhere in south London, who could fix anything. I made an appointment. I had some money, because I worked at weekends and in my holidays, at petrol stations, shops and so on, and took the train to Victoria. The physiotherapist seemed ancient to me, although he was probably only in his early forties, but he was patient and kind. He examined the ankle, announced that I had torn the ligaments and said that it was a pity I had not seen him earlier because there was now considerable scarring. He said that it would take months of special exercises to break this down and build up strength and flexibility in the joint. He gave me a burst of ultrasound to trigger the break up of the scar tissue, and showed me a range of exercises. I was furious: I had been forced to give up football because neither the school nor the Health Service cared if I was a semi-cripple; today this could not happen because sports injuries are treated almost as seriously as any illness or disease. Then, however, doctors did not think it mattered whether you could play a sport; if you could walk, you were fine.

I did my exercises and slowly the ankle grew stronger. But I did not return to football. The years rolled by. I went to Oxford. I became a trainee journalist with the Mirror Group in Plymouth. I still liked sport but now it was running, four miles every evening, half marathons at the weekends, and swimming, thirty lengths most mornings; the ankle was fine now and I could have returned to football but I could not forget the sight of my foot at right angles all those years ago and the pain that followed. Then I moved to London and became a reporter on the *Evening Standard*.

Football had changed. By the late 1970s my heroes from West Ham – Bobby Moore, Martin Peters and Geoff Hurst – had retired. Once players had been older than me; now I would have been a veteran. Brighton had prospered in my absence and were about to be promoted to the First Division. English clubs – stylish Manchester United, robotic Liverpool, and dirty, cheating Leeds – had dominated Europe for much of the decade but, somehow, the game seemed to be decaying, like the whole country. The crowds were angrier, not in the traditional, good-humoured way, but as if they needed Saturday football to give vent to the frustrations of the week.

With American money mainland Europe had been rebuilt after the Second World War but Britain had been bankrupted. We were class-ridden, badly managed and over-unionised; newspapers, for example, paid print workers fortunes for operating obsolete technology because they were terrified of confronting unions with new technology. Management and unions everywhere glowered unproductively at each other. Football was the same. Clubs were run by independently wealthy directors who despised their players and fans and who regarded the game as a socially enhancing hobby.

The election of Margaret Thatcher as Prime Minister in May 1979 was the start of the revolution. She spent the next decade demolishing the old industries and the unions. She was the ultimate free-market capitalist who believed that societies only worked if they were based on self-interest. People who worked hard should be rewarded. Those who did not would sink, and deserved to. There would be so much wealth, however, that the state would be able to afford to maintain this new underclass with benefits. She did not put it as brutally as this but, in essence, that is what she stood for.

She also hated football, because it represented the old Britain of sloppy, amateur management and a dirty working class. Many clubs had drawn support from the industrial working class but Thatcher was destroying them. The stadia had been built a century earlier and were now crumbling safety hazards. Young men, who had once had jobs for life in local factories and had been nourished by extended families, were isolated, unemployed and bitter, and sought the camaraderie of gang warfare on the terraces.

In 1979 I moved to *The Sunday Times*. Under its editor, the brilliant and combative Harold Evans, it had had a momentous decade and had developed new forms of journalism – in investigation, foreign reporting, feature writing and sport – but by the early 1980s it was waiting for a new proprietor who would be ruthless enough to impose new technology.

In 1982 I saw the future of football when *The Sunday Times* sent me to Spain to monitor the English hooligans who were expected to rampage around the country during the World Cup. But there was little trouble – though many reporters, especially from the tabloids, behaved as if Spain was being sacked by barbarians – and I was able to enjoy the magnificent stadia, the crowds, couples and families and the players, who were so much more elegant than their British counterparts. I returned to Spain in 1983 to write a magazine profile of the Argentine genius Diego Maradona, who had just been bought by Barcelona. Again, it was all so much better than in England. The Nou Camp Stadium was sleek and modern; the club was a symbol of Catalan independence as well as being a money-making machine.

I began playing football for *The Sunday Times* in a Fleet Street league. Some newspapers fielded young printers and messengers – the tabloids often turned up with sports columnists who turned out to be ex-internationals – but we managed with only journalists, many of them distinguished men in their own fields, but mostly unfit and terrible at football. Usually we lost heavily but it did not matter; we played on big, artificial pitches, where the ball zipped around, as if we were on fresh, wet grass. I loved it and regretted the lost years. I also played five-a-side every Tuesday evening on a concrete pitch beneath a motorway in west London, alongside future editors and MPs. One grumpy chap later became a multimillionaire economist.

I joined a Sunday park team called Battersea Park, captained by an Irishman who described himself as an actor but who made his living as a painter and decorator. He was a big, handsome man and had once been a good amateur player but he was in his forties now and was slow and heavy, although he still gained enormous pleasure from playing. He told me proudly that his only acting part in recent memory had been in pantomine in Torquay but he had, as he put it, 'chucked it' after a week because Battersea were going 'on tour' in the Low Countries, a euphemism for a pub crawl interrupted by matches against small-town teams on pitches where the goals did not have nets. But it would have been unkind to point this out.

We had a few others like him, once-decent players who had been reduced by age, but most of the team – actors, architects, journalists and solicitors – had always been hopeless. But nothing lasts. Players began to drop away. The goalkeeper's wife had a baby. Our star defender married and began to climb the career ladder at his newspaper. Our midfield general, a journalist who had once played semi-professionally in Hong Kong, got bored. I decided that it was time to quit when we were playing a pub team; most teams in the league were like us, middle class and ageing, but this lot were young, fit, hard and unpleasant. One of them crashed into me and I felt as if I had been hit by a truck. He was a slob; a few years earlier I would have been able to skip past him but those days were gone. It was time to give up before I was seriously injured.

The Sunday Times changed, too. In 1981 Rupert Murdoch, having redefined tabloid journalism at the *Sun*, bought *The Times* and *The Sunday Times*. Evans was lured from his power base at *The Sunday Times* to *The Times* and was soon swept away by Murdoch. The new editor at *The Sunday Times* was Andrew Neil, a fan of Thatcher and Ronald Reagan and all things American. Like Murdoch, he was an outsider who despised the British Establishment for its snobbery, laziness and failure to accept that the country was a decaying mess. Neil sacked many of Evans' ageing writers and recruited the young and ambitious. This was sad but inevitable. It also meant the end of the football team because the new staff were not interested in playing football when they could be networking in Soho wine bars. In 1986 Murdoch smashed the print unions when he moved his newspapers to a high-tech, fortified plant in Wapping, east London, by the Tower of London. The move was necessary but painful; thousands of members of the print unions were fired and many journalists walked out in sympathy and disgust. The Fleet Street league also died that day, amid the bitterness.

Football's nemesis began a year earlier, on the afternoon of 11 May 1985, when the main stand at Valley Parade, home of Bradford City, caught fire. Fifty-six people died as the team, already champions of the Third Division, were all set to receive the acclaim of their long-suffering fans in a game against Lincoln City.

The fire was a disaster waiting to happen. Like many stadia, in all the divisions, Valley Parade was a rotting relic which should have been demolished, or at least rebuilt, many years earlier. The club had planned to replace the stand's wooden roof the following Monday in readiness for the next season in the Second Division but someone dropped a cigarette and the years of accumulated rubbish beneath, which should have been swept up, ignited. Within minutes the stand was a furnace. There were no fences around the pitch; if there had been then many more people would have perished.

The media poured into Bradford. On one level it was a simple story: the stand had been a safety risk and should have been barred to the public. But it was also about the role of football in the new Britain.

Bradford City symbolised what football had once meant to communities. Unbelievable though it was to London sophisticates who endorsed Margaret Thatcher's me-me-me society, the city, battered by the decline of manufacturing industries since the Second World War, had sought hope through its football club. Bradford City had been a formidable force in the early twentieth century but by the 1930s had drifted down to the Third Division (North), where it had remained, losing hope and money, like the city itself. But miraculously it had fought back and on 11 May 1985 was successful and confident.

In the aftermath of the fire the media began to wonder whether football clubs like this had a place in society. Perhaps towns and cities needed a focal point, to unite and energise people; perhaps Thatcher was wrong when she said that Britain consisted of an energetic elite, whose vigour and drive created wealth for the rest. But, if that was so, football would have to modernise. It was not only the physical structures, like Bradford's stand, which needed to be rebuilt; everything had to change.

But a few days later, on 29 May, there was evidence that football did not deserve to be saved. That day Liverpool fans had congregated in Brussels for the evening's European Cup Final against Juventus, due to be played at a crumbling old stadium called the Heysel, which should never have been chosen for a match of this importance and tension. Liverpool's fans were the most widely travelled of British supporters and were certainly not regarded as the most dangerous; although there were hooligans amongst them, for whom football was an opportunity to cause as much trouble as possible, most were genuinely interested in football and were passionate about their club, usually expressed with a sharp Scouse humour. But they did not care for Italians after the previously year's European Cup Final in Rome, when they had been badly treated by the local police, and there were some who were determined to humiliate the Juventus supporters. If this had been England the police would have known this and would have taken extra precautions; grudges between supporters, Manchester United and Leeds, Chelsea and West Ham, Spurs and Arsenal, were common and were dealt with every Saturday throughout the country. But the police in Brussels were more used to handing out parking tickets than dealing with football yobs and their preparations were woeful.

Determined to prove that they were the masters of the Heysel, some Liverpool fans surged towards an area of terracing which should have been occupied by neutrals but which had been taken over by Italians because ticket sales had been a shambles. They broke into the area and, armed with stones, beer cans and fireworks, drove the Italians towards the perimeter fence. A wall collapsed and thirty-nine Italians died. The game was played, because it was thought that it would be more dangerous to call it off, but no one cared about the result. (Juventus won by a single goal.)

As a result of Heysel, English clubs were banned from European competitions for five years – Liverpool for six – which was a statement on how Europeans saw the English. It was as if the Continent was warning England – the Scots, Welsh and Irish were considered quaint, harmless and also blameless – that it was losing patience; either the English learned how to be civilised again or they would be banished. Finally, on the afternoon of 15 April 1989 there was Hillsborough.

That day Liverpool were playing Nottingham Forest in an FA Cup semi-final at Sheffield Wednesday's world-class stadium two miles from the city centre. With only a few minutes before the kick-off, thousands of Liverpool fans were still queuing outside the Leppings Lane terraces, a cramped area which they had been allocated even though everyone had known that Liverpool supporters would easily outnumber Forest's. Then a gate which was meant only to be used for fans leaving the ground was opened and people poured into the centre of the terraces, which, unlike the two ends, were already packed. Men, women and children were crushed against the perimeter fence, a common sight then at grounds after the pitch invasions of the hooligan years; there was no escape as the police and stewards, inured to the idea that football crowds could only cause trouble, thought that a riot had broken out.

Ninety-five people died that afternoon and hundreds more were injured and traumatised.

South Yorkshire police blamed the fans, most disgracefully in a briefing to the *Sun*. The story was a farrago of lies and half-truths and should have led, at the very least, to the dismissal of the newspaper's high command; instead the city of Liverpool took action by boycotting the newspaper. At first the rest of the media took a similarly critical, if more restrained, line. This was understandable since reporters were talking to spokespeople from respected organisations, such as the police and Sheffield Wednesday. But the media, whatever its faults, can usually sniff a lie and soon the real story – of police incompetence followed by cover-up – began to dribble out. Ordinary, decent people had died at Hillsborough, not drunken yobs.

The Taylor Report into football was published on 18 January 1990 and contained dozens of recommendations – such as replacing terraces with seats, removing perimeter fences and installing closed circuit television at grounds – but it was basically a demand for the sport to modernise or die. Football was now a business, which had responsibilities to its customers, and, if it could not satisfy these, then it had no right to exist.

The Wapping revolution meant that newspapers could now be produced without highly paid printers. This led to the creation of the *Independent* and then the *Sunday Correspondent*, which I joined in the summer of 1989. It only survived a year. The economy was slumping and advertising dropped. The *Independent*, piqued that another freestanding group of hacks had moved into what had always been a lucrative market, launched a Sunday newspaper. *The Sunday Times*, *Observer* and *Sunday Telegraph*, with more money and more resources, improved. Thus, the *Sunday Correspondent*, which was honest and solid without ever being inspired, collapsed.

It did, however, have enough money to send me to the World Cup in Italy in 1990, once again to report on English hooligans or rather, since this was a serious broadsheet newspaper, to comment on how British tabloids sensationalised the threat posed by English fans. I knew from the World Cup in Spain eight years earlier that hooliganism by England supporters had always been exaggerated; at worst, there had only ever been a few hundred thugs from the most notorious clubs, such as Millwall, West Ham, Chelsea and Leeds, who united briefly and resentfully under the flag of St George. Compared with the orchestrated battles at home between these 'firms', violence abroad by supporters of the national team had been sporadic but even these days were over.

I described how the island of Sardinia, where England had been corralled for the first stage by the Italian organisers, reacted to the ugly, pot-bellied, tattooed and shaven-haired English creatures, who hung around the streets pretending to be 'up for it'. There were a few scuffles with local yobs but the tabloid hacks filed the stories their editors wanted. So, according to these newspapers, Sardinia resembled a war zone. It was rubbish and showed that these newspapers, whose natural audience includes the yobs they were writing about, often invented hooliganism to boost sales, while, at the same time, condemning it.

Then England qualified for the second stage and we joined the World Cup on the mainland. These were wonderful weeks. First, England beat Belgium 1-0 in Bologna. They played beautiful but violent Cameroon in Naples and won a sublime match 3-2. Finally, it was the West Germans in the semi-final in Turin. With 30 million people watching in Britain on television this was the night football became the sport fit for a country which had finally forgotten the past. England lost after a penalty shoot-out but that was irrelevant. The World Cup had shown that football was stylish and fun; it was played in gorgeous stadia by tanned young men, cheered on by tens of thousands of middle-class enthusiasts. It was no longer grainy black and white, violent and grim.

It only required someone to explain why football mattered. And in 1992 Nick Hornby did that brilliantly. Football's new fans now had a guru but Hornby was not like them. He did not think that football was an athletic version of Glyndebourne. He did not see himself as a customer. His relationship with Arsenal did not depend on nice seats and first-class snacks at half-time; it was passionate, complicated and often unhappy. But that was not what the new fans wanted to hear. They bought his book and quoted it to each other over dinner but they did not understand what he was saying.

Chapter Four

The Governors

In October 1999 the Football Association appointed Adam Crozier as its new chief executive. Crozier, a thirty-five-year-old advertising executive, was supposed to herald the transformation of the FA from an anachronistic joke to a modern organisation capable of managing a sport which had become a multimillion pound industry. Alas, the FA managed to botch the task of replacing Graham Kelly, a dull bureaucrat who had been forced to resign after unpleasantness involving a loan to the Welsh Football Association.

After employing expensive head-hunters to locate a suitable person to lead them into the next millennium, the FA chose Crozier, then chief executive at Saatchi and Saatchi, partly because he knew a lot about football – he had once played for the youth team of a Scottish club – but mainly because he was a brilliant businessman. The FA said that it did not matter that he was Scottish, and insisted that he was the man for the job. But then a newspaper revealed that Crozier had fiddled his sales figures when he was selling advertising space at the *Daily Telegraph*. Crozier apologised for his 'youthful error' but the damage had already been done; the FA always made a hash of everything.

In theory the FA is responsible for all football throughout England: Premier League giants, semi-professional, amateur and children's leagues all have to report to Lancaster Gate. Above the FA is the organisation governing football in Europe, the Union of European Football Associations (UEFA) and, finally, there is FIFA, Fédération Internationale de Football Associations, football's equivalent to the US Supreme Court or the Law Lords in England. But it is hard to find anyone in football – chairmen, managers, players or fans – with a kind word to say about the FA. It exists *because* it exists; its only function is to find reasons to continue. Football could survive happily and, indeed, would be better off without it.

The FA was formed in autumn 1863 when eleven clubs met in London in the Freemason's Tavern on Great Queen Street to bring order to a sport which did not have an agreed set of rules. After four more meetings these pioneers had reached agreement and issued the proclamation that created modern football. Only Crystal Palace survive on today's pools coupons from this band; the rest – Barnes, Blackheath, Charterhouse, Perceval House, Kensington School, War Office, Blackheath Proprietary School, The Crusaders, Forest and No Names, of Kilburn, north-west London – have vanished.

Football boomed, especially in the industrial heartlands, where it became the escape every Saturday afternoon for factory workers. As the game became more popular so did professionalism; in 1885 the FA reluctantly authorised what was already a fact, that players could be paid. But matches between the leading clubs were irregular and had no point to them other than pride. Thus, in spring 1888, William McGregor, a Scot who had become a successful businessman in Birmingham and an official at Aston Villa, summoned the top clubs to organise a league which would be modelled on baseball's National League in the United States, which had been set up in 1876.

The meeting took place at Anderton's Hotel in Fleet Street, London, on 22 March. Six of the clubs which sent representatives to the hotel came from the North-West – Accrington Stanley, Blackburn Rovers, Bolton Wanderers, Burnley, Everton and Preston North End – while the rest – Aston Villa, Derby County,

Notts County, Stoke City, West Bromwich Albion and Wolverhampton Wanderers – came from the Midlands. The following month the clubs met again in Manchester and decided to call the new organisation the Football League.

For the next century the FA and the Football League coexisted unhappily. The FA was the arbiter of football in England, exacted punishments and controlled the national teams while the league organised the leading professional clubs into four divisions. By the late 1980s, however, the top clubs in the Football League's First Division were restless. The game here was on the brink of a transformation from a hooligan-ravaged, near-bankrupt recreation for the working class into a multimillion pound extension of show business; the major clubs thought that they should control their own destinies and said that it was absurd that they should have to listen to the Football League and the also-rans of the lower divisions. They also argued that they should not have to share their profits with the proletariat of professional football since the fans and the television companies were only interested in them.

This was a substantial argument and one which delighted the FA, long resentful of the Football League. In the aftermath of the World Cup in Italy in 1990, as sponsors and satellite television moved in to exploit the sport, the Football League tried to save itself by drawing up a plan; entitled 'One Game, One Team, One Voice', it proposed that a new organisation, a council made up of representatives from the League and the FA, should control professional football.

The FA, however, was not interested in an alliance and revealed its own 'blueprint'; this proposed that the First Division clubs form a Premier League, which would be independent commercially but which would acknowledge the authority of the association. The FA bragged that the formation of this elite league in 1992 proved that it had taken hold of the richest slice of the football cake; it did not occur to anyone at the FA that the Premier League could manage without the FA, just as it could manage without the Football League.

It could be argued that market forces – that the giant clubs which generated hundreds of millions every year would inevitably demand independence from clubs which needed local sponsors to buy match balls – would have destroyed the unity of the Football League, but even by its own standards it was staggeringly stupid of the FA to believe that it would be able to control the Premier League. It did not take long for the FA to realise its mistake: within a few months the bureaucrats at Lancaster Gate were squealing that the Premier League was behaving as if the FA was irrelevant, which is precisely what the chairmen of the major clubs thought.

A few years ago, when Graham Kelly was still chief executive, a magazine asked me to investigate the FA, hoping that I would find evidence of criminal wrongdoing rather than the incompetence which had long been its public face. After interviewing bureaucrats like Kelly, elected officials, chairmen of major clubs and football writers, I found no evidence of any criminal acitvity and concluded that the FA had simply outlived its usefulness and deserved to be put out of its misery.

Like most organisations, the FA is stubborn. It is run by men (most women at the FA occupy humble positions because football remains overwhelmingly male) who earn handsome salaries and do not see why they should abolish themselves. They report to ancient chaps in blazers, who like the status of being on FA committees and the perks which come with this, such as complimentary seats, blankets and half-time sandwiches at cup finals.

But the forces of revolution are gaining strength. The money-making machines of the Premier League do not want to pay homage to the FA; the journeymen clubs of the Football League have their own governing body and cannot be bothered with the FA; beneath them are thousands of smaller clubs, from well-run, semi-professional teams with neat stadia and dreams of moving into the big time to pub sides who turn out on park pitches strewn with dog mess. Most complain that the FA's only purpose is to collect subscriptions, levy fines and make a nuisance of itself.

The Governors

The FA is based in a stuccoed terrace at Lancaster Gate, on the north side of Hyde Park. Apart from the hushed voices of the telephonists, the reception room is silent, like a cathedral. Flags, shields and cups are displayed in glass cabinets. There are faded photographs of strapping men, wearing walrus moustaches, baggy shorts and heavy boots. These were the gentlemen amateurs, who played for love not money. Next are the photographs from the 1880s – hard men from the North and the Midlands, the first professionals, who kicked lumps out of each other for a few shillings. It was not much, even then, but it was preferable to breathing in coal dust in a mine.

There are pictures of the England team who beat West Germany 4–2 in the World Cup Final at Wembley in 1966. The late Bobby Moore, the golden-haired captain, is there, immortalised in his youth and glory. Bobby Charlton, wisps of hair plastered with sweat across his forehead, is in mid-air, alongside Nobby Stiles, ferocious and toothless, and Superman-lookalike Geoff Hurst, whose goal in extra-time – turn, smash, the ball hits the bar and bounces down and out, but did it cross the line? – is the source of one of sport's enduring and unprovable arguments. But these legends seem dated today: the shirts and shorts are too tight and their bodies too slender.

And there are photographs of today's stars. They have the muscled bodies, styled hair and capped teeth of contemporary professional super-athletes. They earn millions from their clubs and from advertising and sponsorship, live in mansions, protected from the public by the latest security devices, drive James Bond cars, and, providing that they take the advice of their accountants, spend their retirement thumping golf balls in Spain. They wear billowing shirts which fans buy for extortionate sums because they want to identify with their clubs or because they think that wearing these fashion disasters means that they are David Beckham.

The daily newspapers are laid out on a coffee table, testifying to football's hold on the national psyche. Other sports – tennis, rugby, horse racing – are covered in detail, because sport sells newspapers, but football occupies more space than the rest put together. In the broadsheets there are thoughtful articles analysing Chelsea's deployment of wing backs and Middlesbrough's reliance on their new Brazilian midfield dynamo, as if football is as important and complex as global warming. The middle-market newspapers run exposés of the inadequacies of teams and managers, and the tabloids run ghost-written critiques by ex-players on current ones.

There are stacks of glossy brochures advertising FA courses for coaches, referees, physiotherapists and doctors, and piles of postcards, with the grinning image of the England manager. (Glenn Hoddle was the incumbent when I visited, but he was sacked soon afterwards when he shared his ideas on reincarnation with the nation.) There are also piles of documents detailing the annual accounts of the FA and describing how this non-profit-making organisation has saved the professional game. The figures are mind-boggling rows of noughts. Football is awash with money and even the bumbling FA has managed to benefit: its turnover has soared by £20 million in four years and is nudging £55 million annually, of which £20 million comes from television and £10 million from assorted commercial activities in conjunction with what the FA calls its 'family of sponsors', as if multinational companies cared about anything apart from balance sheets.

The FA's salary bill for the one hundred and thirty or so staff is around £5 million a year, but, as is the way with post-Thatcherite organisations, the bulk of this goes to the senior men. It is also spending £10 million in an attempt to convince FIFA to award the World Cup of 2006 to England, thus breaking a pledge to the Germans that it would back them, in return for Germany's help in persuading UEFA to stage the European Championship in 1996 in England.

Ushered upstairs to meet Graham Kelly, I thought that anyone running such a massive organisation could not possibly be as third rate as the media suggested. I flicked through my newspaper clippings on the FA to check that I knew what to ask him, and spotted an interview with Sir Bert Millichip, then in his eighties, and the FA's former chairman. Sir Bert was not happy. He said that he was worried about 'hooliganism, drug abuse, financial irregularities [at the clubs] and discipline'. Football, like real life, was a never-ending challenge: 'Every time we solved one problem, another two seemed to arrive on the table,' he said recently. Sir Bert might, I thought, be old but he is realistic.

There was more. The leading Premier League clubs are international brand names who want to negotiate pay-per-view deals with broadcasting moguls. Beneath them are the lesser Premier League clubs, bankrupting themselves by paying huge salaries to players who might be able to keep them in the only league which matters, and, below them, the Nationwide League clubs, most of whom are tottering perpetually on the edge of extinction.

As I knocked on Kelly's door, the thought occurred to me: what is the FA *for*? It runs the national teams and organises football outside the senior professional levels. Its bureaucrats, like Kelly, report to dozens of committees, consisting of elderly gents who reminisce about their glory days in Corinthian local football, and an FA council, made up of ninety-one men and one woman, which potters along, deciding nothing over tea and sandwiches. Would it matter if the FA vanished? The professional leagues would carry on, as they were doing. The FA Cup and England teams could be managed by wizards in marketing and television rights, though they might not have to worry about the FA Cup for much longer; the competition is withering because the giants of football, such as Manchester United, have decided that European and global competitions offer more opportunities for making money than an English knockout, which involves playing rough and disrespectful little teams.

Kelly was unwilling to address the big issues facing the FA. Every question, no matter how provocative, was met with the same lugubrious expression, evidence that the FA's recently installed public relations supremo, a former BBC television reporter called

David Davies, had taught him how to avoid making a complete fool of himself. This was a pity: because once you could rely on Kelly to relieve the tedium of his own personality by saying something stupid about whatever scandal – drugs, bribery, hooliganism – was rocking football. But those days were over.

I tried everything. I asked him if the FA was a gravy train for people like him, who travelled the world Business Class, attending meaningless meetings. He considered this proposition, smiled feebly and said that, on balance, taking all things into account, everyone at the FA worked jolly hard and deserved to be properly remunerated. Then I lobbed the word 'bung' – footballspeak for managers taking bribes from agents who broker transfers – at him. Surely George Graham, sacked as Arsenal manager in 1995 after it was revealed that he had taken 'unsolicited gifts' from a Norwegian agent – was not the only crooked manager? Kelly mumbled that 'things have been tightened up considerably' since the Graham affair. What about Terry Venables, the England manager who complained that he had been forced to resign by the FA in 1996 because of his long-running legal battle with his former chairman Alan Sugar, the founder of Amstrad, which dated from their unhappy partnership at Tottenham? Surely the FA should have backed Venables, who might have had a patchy record in business but who remained a first-rate coach? Oh no, said Kelly, that is not the case at all. Football is about passion and people tend to get 'worked up'; 'Anyway,' he added with the self-serving non sequitur which is common in football, 'I was keen for Terry to stay on.'

Kelly's office contained a desk, two telephones, a few files and a bottle of mineral water. He was a large man who controlled his weight by early morning jogging, lunchtime five-a-side football in Hyde Park and occasional diets. He was wearing a grey suit, quiet tie and spectacles; if you bumped into him at one of the lower division league games which he enjoyed attending you might have mistaken him for a bank manager reaching the end of a disappointing career. He had dreamt of becoming a professional goalkeeper but was not good enough and decided that banking offered a steady, clean career. (His father had been a tram driver and his mother a barmaid.) He began his ascent of football's administrative ladder in 1968 when he joined the Football League at Lytham St Anne's, near his home in Blackpool, and arrived at the FA as chief executive in February 1989.

When I met him he was reportedly earning £150,000. (A few months after Kelly's departure in December 1998, however, Howard Wilkinson, the grumpy, aloof, former manager of Leeds United and Sheffield Wednesday was earning £300,000 as the FA's 'technical director' with a brief to save English football. Kevin Keegan was later offered £900,000 to become England coach.) Kelly had also suffered unrelenting criticism from the media and had become the symbol of everything that was wrong with English football: dim, clumsy and devoid of flair. My file of newspaper clippings bulged with profiles describing him as a buffoon. They pointed out that England had not won a trophy since 1966 and that successive England managers had been appointed, amidst great hype, by the FA, only to be unceremoniously dumped. Football writers had told me that Kelly was a decent bloke, though they could not say that in print, since the public needed a scapegoat for England's decline as a world power; they thought that he had been overpromoted from his natural position, which lay somewhere in the powerless middle regions of a bureaucracy.

Newspapers had tried occasionally to turn him into a colourful figure. One had revealed that after 24 years of marriage he had left his wife – and two children – and set up home near Peterborough with another man's wife. But this story – which was supposed to be 'the sex scandal of Britain's top soccer boss' – flopped. This was not surprising since the newspaper pointed out that Kelly was known as Mr Boring and that his mistress was 'dumpy and middle aged'.

It was obvious that Kelly did not think that it was his job to tackle the fundamental problems facing football. He was the bureaucrat who did what he was told by the FA's elected officials and it was too bad if they did not have the brains or courage to sort out football. He would continue to collect his salary, jet around the world meeting other bureaucrats and pull balls out of a bag at televised FA Cup draws.

I asked him if he thought that the FA was redundant. He frowned. Every sport needs a governing body, he mumbled. Err, if the FA didn't exist, there would be anarchy.

It was easy to sympathise with the Premiership clubs because the FA council was full of men who could talk knowledgeably about, say, the difficulties of fitting nets to goal posts on park pitches but who were ignorant about the mechanics of running multinational businesses, which is what clubs had become.

This council was a bizarre body, sport's equivalent of the unreformed House of Lords. The council was white and, with one exception (a thirty-six-year-old who spoke for the Women's Football Alliance), male. Most members were old: six were in their eighties, twenty in their seventies and thirty-nine in their sixties. There were two youngsters, both in their thirties. Twenty came from the professional game, and a handful from the Premier League, but the majority belonged to amateur organisations in the counties. The rest came from the Army, Navy and Air Force, the universities and schools. The council provided the personnel for the FA's committees, which bureaucrats like Kelly reported to. There were twenty such committees, dealing with referees, cups, leagues, discipline and so on. There was even one dedicated to revising the rules under which other committees operated.

A few council members could see that this was a nonsense. A solicitor named Frank Pattison, representing Durham, told me that as a sixty year old he was a 'comparatively young fart' by the standards of the FA. Pattison obviously loved the sport – he had been president of the Durham FA since 1984 and a member of the FA council since 1989 – and agreed that his colleagues, though they were 'good men', might not be the best people to run the new football. Pattison thought that the council should transfer many of its powers to a board of management, composed of a few FA council members and professionals who knew about making money.

But many did not agree. David Henson, a fifty-six-year-old antique dealer and owner of a bed and breakfast establishment, was Devon's voice within the FA. He thought that FA bureaucrats needed to be monitored by men like him to ensure that they did not forget the grass roots. He was particularly worried that the Premier League, which 'only cares about money', would soon dominate Lancaster Gate.

The most vocal critics of the FA amongst Premier League chairmen were Chelsea's Ken Bates and Newcastle's Sir John Hall, but neither would speak to me, which was a shame since these two men were responsible for transforming the landscape of top-flight football. Bates, irascible and vain but totally committed to Chelsea, was building a giant to rival Manchester United by capitalising on the club's position in one of the most fashionable areas of London; like the great continental clubs, such as Barcelona, he wanted Chelsea to be an industry, with hotels, apartments, restaurants and a club superstore, as well as a cosmopolitan team which would appeal to sponsors around the world. Hall, on the other hand, was attempting to use football to tug the North East out of the depression which followed the dismantling of heavy industry; he was saying to Geordies, 'look, if Newcastle United can make it then so can you'. The logic was dubious – since Hall was spending tens of millions of his own money at United – but you had to admire him for trying.

But Alan Sugar, the Spurs chairman, was delighted to tell me what he thought of the FA. Over tea at the office of his public relations advisers in central London, Sugar, wearing *Miami Vice*-style stubble and a beautiful suit, fizzed with rage: 'They are a load of fuddy-duddies who are protecting their own power. You've got to disband the whole bloody thing and start again. Graham Kelly is just the bloke who is the chief executive of this albatross.' He added that the FA was irrelevant to the Premier League. 'We could say, bollocks to the lot of you. We could run our league. We would be chucked out of European competitions but they'd soon realise that they needed us.'

Sugar's irritation was understandable. The FA had stumbled from disaster to fiasco and back again. England managers came and went, exhausted by the failure to produce the world-beating teams which the media demanded. Bobby Robson did better than most and was a penalty shoot-out away from a World Cup Final in Italy in 1990, but that had not saved him. It was business as usual after that: Graham Taylor was decent but limited; Terry Venables was brilliant but had disastrous ambitions to be a tycoon; Glenn Hoddle had been a marvellous player but was a poor manager, though it was his betrayal of his players in a ghost-written World Cup diary and his dabbling in New Age philosophy that finally destroyed him. The FA had appointed David Davies to try and modernise its lamentable public relations. Davies had done well but had been helpless during the run up to the European Championship in England in 1996.

On the eve of the competition Trevor Phillips, the FA's commercial director for the previous seven years, resigned. His exit was followed by headlines about dodgy ticket sales and police undercover operations which suggested, without actually saying so since that would have been libellous, that he was lucky to be a free man. Kelly was summoned by the media to appear on the steps of Lancaster Gate, where he always stood in moments of crisis, to do his impression of a man who had just been told that he had a few hours to live. But he said that he could not discuss Phillips because police enquiries were continuing.

I tracked Phillips down to Johannesburg, where he was responsible for turning football from what had been a chaotic black township game under apartheid into a mainstream sport. The South Africans wanted to host the 2006 World Cup and it was essential that their domestic leagues were properly organised. Phillips was the chief executive of the country's new premier league, which proved that the South Africans regarded him as honest and competent. At first he refused to discuss the FA because, he said, he 'always got screwed by journalists'; then he cited the confidentiality agreement which he had signed with the FA in return for a severance cheque. I pressed on. Had he been questioned by the police? Silence. Then, 'Yes'. Had he been sacked? 'I resigned, but I wasn't sorry to go.' Who wanted him out? 'The FA just dropped me.' Then I asked him the Big Question. What is the FA *for*? He snapped and, presumably realising that the FA would hardly chase him to South Africa for the return of his payoff, said that he had no idea. 'I spent all my time there trying to work it out. The only concern they have is protocol, getting in the right seat or into the Royal Box at Wembley.'

And this was just the start. For half an hour Phillips, now in his mid-fifties, raged about the FA. He said that the saga which led to his departure began in 1993, when England were awarded Euro '96 by UEFA. Phillips and Glenn Kirton, an FA stalwart since 1971, had begun preparing for the event which would signal that football in England was now a respectable industry. Stadia were improved, hotels made ready for an invasion of overseas fans. Security was tightened. Meanwhile, Phillips tried to sell 1.4 million tickets. He told me that this had been tricky because of UEFA regulations covering the distribution of seats to competing nations and the various deals which the FA, as hosts, had struck with companies which wanted a slice of the Euro-bonanza. He said: 'The politicians in football bid for these big competitions but they do not understand the financial constraints on the hosts, who have to bear all the costs. We calculated that we had to sell 85 per cent of the tickets to break even.' About 10 per cent of tickets were supposed to be sold to fans abroad, with the remainder destined for English supporters. But business had been slow and Phillips fretted that he would be left with thousands of unsold tickets. The FA had decreed that only two companies could sell 'corporate hospitality packages' – which is the way that contemporary sport describes tickets flogged for many times their face value because car parking passes and bad lunches are thrown in. Phillips had decided to widen the net. 'I thought that we should use a wider spread of companies. I knew that I was going against FA policy and told them what I was doing.'

The details of how he defied his masters at the FA are unimportant – the fact that the police did not pursue him shows that he did not do anything illegal – but he was forced to leave Lancaster Gate. *The Financial Times*, a newspaper not prone to hyperbole, summed up the disaster: 'The Euro '96 ticket scandal rocking the Football Association was looking last night like a gross management error rather than criminal scandal. A police investigation over several months turned out to be based on misleading information from the FA and resulted in Scotland Yard's statement in effect criticising the FA for not knowing its right foot from its left.'

Phillips had recovered from what could have been a terminal career setback but was furious at his treatment. Euro '96, which he had helped mastermind, generated £100 million. About £50 million was spent organising the tournament; the rest went to UEFA and the sixteen competing countries. Phillips said, 'I was annoyed that I had to watch from the sidelines. I had taken the income of the FA from £6 million a year to over £40 million. It was a hard struggle, trying to commercialise an animal that had no understanding of the market place.'

Phillips' career and dismissal summed up the unresolved conflicts within the FA: an organisation which remained amateur at heart was attempting to control a complex and lucrative business. Phillips recalled his meetings with the committees which monitored his activities: 'I could see their eyes glaze over when I talked about marketing. What do these people know about the modern game at the top level? The FA Council only had one purpose: to prevent change. I used to feel like saying, let's all join hands and try and contact the living.'

The FA did not heed the warning of the Phillips fiasco. As far as it was concerned he had broken the rules and been punished.

Certainly, the money continued to pour into Lancaster Gate. Phil Carling, a bright and affable man from Arsenal, succeeded Phillips and, by summer 1998, as England prepared for the World Cup in France, reported more heartening results. Turnover at the FA was soaring, thanks to television's insatiable interest. So busy was Carling that his department had doubled in size, from five to ten, since his appointment. Surely, the FA argued, no one can criticise us again for being unprofessional.

But the problems which Kelly had refused to acknowledge began to tear apart the organisation in the late 1990s.

First came the World Cup in France in 1998, when Glenn Hoddle's team managed to scrape into the second round, courtesy of Michael Owen, a Liverpudlian who looked like a choir boy, before being beaten by Argentina. This match was remarkable only because it revealed the self-delusion which infected manager, players, officials and media. England were an ordinary team, with a couple of world-class performers, David Beckham and now Owen, and had no right to expect to progress in the tournament. But the Premier League markets itself as the best in the world and everyone connected professionally with the game shares in the myth; if they did not, they would have to tell the truth, that the English players in the league are no better than the men who used to drive second-hand cars and worried about their mortgages.

Defeat in France was also the beginning of the end for Hoddle. He published his diary of the competition, ghost-written by David Davies. Apart from confirming that Hoddle was self-obsessed and muddle-headed, it was also a betrayal of his team. But Hoddle was so sure of his superiority, and so contemptuous of his players, that he revealed everything, which was like a wife going on a chat show and criticising her husband's sexual performance.

The book, which was serialised in a tabloid newspaper, should have led to his sacking, but the FA hung on, desperate to avoid losing another England boss so soon after the departure of Terry Venables.

Kelly defended Hoddle, which was predictable since he was Kelly's man. Then Kelly fell in December 1998, when it emerged that with Keith Wiseman, a solicitor and coroner from Southampton, who was the FA's chairman (he managed to make Kelly seem charismatic), he had lobbied too enthusiastically for the FA to be represented on an elite committee within FIFA.

A few weeks later Hoddle also departed after he speculated that handicapped people were being punished for sins committed in an earlier life. Reincarnation is a central tenet of many religions but it is not the job of a football manager to talk about it; after the World Cup diary, and Hoddle's fascination with a faith healer, this was too much for the media, who were bored with his ramblings, and the FA was forced to fire him.

The organisation was now officially a shambles. It had lost its chief executive, chairman and the latest, failed saviour of the national team. David Davies dreamt of replacing Kelly but, forever tarnished by his association with Hoddle's diary, had no chance.

While contenders for the vacant positions at Lancaster Gate lobbied and briefed slyly against each other, the Premier League also self-destructed. It lost its chief executive, Peter Leaver, a barrister, and its chairman, Sir John Quinton, a former banker, in a row over the only thing that the clubs really cared about: money. Leaver, who had already irritated the giants by refusing to back their plans for a European super-league, had agreed to pay extraordinary amounts to two ex-Sky executives, Sam Chisholm and David Chance, if they negotiated lucrative new deals when the existing contracts expired in 2001. The details of the contracts were staggering. The most decrepit member of the FA council could have extracted more cash from television since football was the most important ingredient in the ratings battles raging between terrestrial, satellite, cable and digital channels. But, for unknown reasons, Leaver had agreed to pay Chisholm and Chance annual retainers of £650,000 each, with bonuses which would have totalled tens of millions if Sky, which was already paying £743 million over five years, was willing to spend over £1 billion for another five years. The Premier League clubs might have privately admired Chisholm and Chance for pulling off such a spectacular deal but they had no intention of allowing Leaver and Quinton, the two men responsible for wasting their money, to survive.

The campaign for the FA chairmanship was portrayed by the media as a battle between a professional who was a moderniser and a stalwart amateur who believed in discipline. The former was David Sheepshanks, a forty-six-year-old food tycoon who was sleek and well-groomed and who made the kind of punchy, let's-do-it speeches favoured by politicians, while aides whispered background guidance to hacks. Sheepshanks, the Old Etonian chairman of Ipswich Town and former chairman of the Football League, said that he would share the money from television more equitably – this did not worry the Premier League clubs since they knew that the FA could not force them to do any such thing – and stem the influx of European players – which was a meaningless promise since freedom of labour is an intrinsic part of the European Union. His rival, Geoff Thompson, a magistrate from Sheffield, was portrayed as a traditionalist, whose main support came from the amateur game. But, on closer examination, his manifesto did not differ much from Sheepshanks'; Thompson also talked about the need for the FA and Premier and Football Leagues to work together, about the necessity of a successful national team, about the desirability of England staging the World Cup and finally, about transferring many of the powers of the FA council to small committees which could make decisions quickly.

Thanks to his friends in the counties and within the Premier League, Thompson won easily. As the first salaried (£50,000 per year) chairman of the FA he swung into action. The council were told that they would have to forfeit power to a board of directors, composed of six representatives from the professional game and six from the amateur, with the chairman and chief executive holding non-voting seats. Thompson extracted from the Premier League the sum of £12 million a year for ten years to fund the sport at 'grass roots', which cynics dismissed as a ploy by the giants to buy silence from the FA as they continued their remorseless expansion at the expense of the Football League.

But these reforms were cosmetic because they did not address the fundamental issue: should the FA exist? Common sense suggested that the FA should abolish itself since it had lost authority over the professional game and was despised by the amateurs. The professional game was run by the Premier League and Football League, who saw the FA as an irritating irrelevance, which tried to justify itself by constantly issuing edicts on the rules of the game. To amateurs Lancaster Gate was the organisation which collected money and did nothing in return.

But the FA lumbered on. It insisted that England would be an excellent host for the World Cup in 2006, despite its pledge to Germany that it would not bid for the competition and, more important, despite the fact that the South Africans needed the event more than two wealthy European countries. If the FA had been interested in anything other than money it would have abandoned its campaign and backed the South Africans, for whom a World Cup would mean investment in stadia, transport, communications and security. It would be naive to pretend that was the reason South Africa had such widespread support within FIFA: FIFA smelt marketing opportunities in black Africa, just as it had done when it awarded the 1994 World Cup to the United States, but justice definitely decreed that the competition should go to the continent for the first time.

Kelly, meanwhile, had popped up again, like a bad dream. He published his memoirs, *Sweet FA*, which confirmed him as football's Mr Nobody, who had prospered at Lancaster Gate because he was a pompous bureaucrat. Much of the book was taken up with descriptions of his travels to Antigua, Paraguay, the south of France and so on in his capacity as 'chief executive of the mother nation of football'. Sometimes there were really serious crises. Kelly recalled that he had been dining in Zürich with Sepp Blatter, general secretary of FIFA – 'It was my turn to pay but, unfortunately, the restaurant did not acknowledge any of my credit cards,' Kelly confided.

Newspapers were excited by his mini-revelations. He recalled how Alan Shearer, the England captain, had threatened to pull out of the World Cup squad in 1998 if the FA investigated an incident when Shearer's Newcastle United were playing Leicester City. He also recounted the curious case of the vanishing Ruud Gullit, the Dutch midfield genius who had moved into management, first with Chelsea and then with Newcastle. Kelly said that Gullit's agent had told the FA that his client wanted to have a chat about the job vacated by Hoddle. Kelly had agreed and had waited for the great man to arrive. But, despite repeated messages charting Gullit's progress through London traffic, he never appeared. Oh well, concluded Kelly, life's a funny old business, isn't it?

The overwhelming impression of *Sweet FA* was of an organisation bereft of intelligence where senior staff were only concerned about their status. Kelly remembered his first meeting with Hoddle, the people's choice to succeed Venables: 'We discussed the possibility of a four-year contract before getting into a rather esoteric conversation about the relative values of reflexology and spiritual healing.' It did not occur to Kelly or anyone else at the FA that an England coach who was interested in such matters might, perhaps, not be treated sympathetically by the media or his players.

UEFA, which was founded in 1954, and FIFA, which began life in 1904, both based in comfy Switzerland, were no more impressive than the FA as the twentieth century ambled to a close.

UEFA failed to understand that the balance of power had shifted away from the national teams and towards the major European clubs. These were stupendously wealthy, thanks to television, and were able to pay enormous transfer fees and salaries to players. It followed from this that they were increasingly reluctant to release these valuable 'properties' for international fixtures.

UEFA decided, therefore, to make as much money as quickly as possible, by expanding its competitions for clubs; the European

Cup, which had once been contested by the elite, became a meandering joke. UEFA also tried to squeeze more cash out of its tournament for national teams, the European Championship, by inviting any independent European country with eleven able-bodied men to compete.

The European Cup, once a thrilling knockout tournament between Europe's best teams, had become the Champions' League. But most of the teams competing in it were not champions of anything. The leading countries, such as England, were able to enter two or three clubs while the minnows, mainly from the new states of Eastern Europe and the former Soviet Union, dispatched teams which would have struggled in an English semi-professional league. But television needed lots of teams to play lots of matches; then, when the no-hopers had been eliminated, the real competition could start with more mini leagues. Finally, there would be a knockout, by which time UEFA and the clubs would have made fortunes.

UEFA's secondary competitions – once honourable events for the winners of domestic cups and runners-up in the most competitive leagues – were totally devalued. Ninety-two teams were involved in the new UEFA Cup, many of whom would have fitted in nicely on a Sunday morning on Hackney Marshes. But UEFA did not care.

Money was one factor; fear was another. UEFA had been desperate to prevent the major European teams forming a super-league, which would destroy its own cups, so it had bought off the clubs with expanded competitions, no matter what the cost to the domestic leagues in the individual countries and even though this surfeit of over-hyped football would inevitably alienate the public.

Once, baffled by the number of games, I telephoned UEFA to find out how the Champions' League, the UEFA Cup and the Inter-Toto Cup were organised. Ah, that's not easy to answer, said a press officer; it would be best to fax the flow charts and tables, explaining how teams qualified for each event and how they would move from one to another during the season, depending on how they performed. The fax was an incomprehensible jumble so I tried again. Right, said the press officer, it works like this. Every country has a ranking. The higher you are then the more teams you can enter in the Champions' League. Teams which fail to qualify for the final stages of the competition can go to the UEFA Cup, which begins with one hundred and twenty-one teams. But once again the number of teams from each country, and the point at which they joined the event, depends on the rankings. Then he moved to the Inter-Toto but by now I did not care about the details, which were so complex that it required a degree in mathematics to understand them. So, I said, it's all about more matches and more money. Yes, he replied, that's right.

Some former players spoke out against this. Johan Cruyff, the legendary Dutch star, said that the first stage of the cup did not interest him. 'It has been changed to make more money. The competition has been decaffeinated [sic].'

UEFA also increased the size of the European Championship for national teams. This was partly forced on them by the break up of the old Communist states – Yugoslavia fractured into four countries: Slovenia, Bosnia-Herzegovina, Croatia and Serbian-run Yugoslavia – but it was also the result of greed: the bigger a competition the more money could be made from it. So there were dozens of matches involving football nonentities such as the Faroe Islands and Andorra, where crowds were measured in the hundreds, before the real tournament began in Holland and Belgium in summer 2000.

The mounting power of clubs also threatened FIFA so, in an attempt to justify itself, it courted the Third World by expanding an already bloated World Cup. Senior FIFA figures also endorsed South Africa's bid for 2006; this would have been laudable if they had done so out of a desire to help black South Africans, but it was a cynical ploy, which had everything to do with FIFA's internal politics and nothing to do with boosting black Africa's self-respect.

FIFA even launched its own club competition, the World Club Championship, a ridiculous concoction for continental champions, in South America early in 2000. This led to the withdrawal of Manchester United, as European champions, from the FA Cup because the British Government thought that it would damage England's bid for the 2006 World Cup if United did not take part.

Meanwhile, UEFA and FIFA argued with each other about the shape of football in the next century. Publicly they claimed that they wanted to curb commercialism, the monstrous transfer fees and salaries which were pushing football towards financial oblivion, and the number of matches being played, which were exhausting players and boring the public. FIFA's general secretary, Michel Zen-Ruffinen, led the hypocrisy league table. He said that UEFA had gone too far; the Champions' League had too many games and the UEFA Cup was 'a fiasco'. He said, 'There is a risk of saturation in top-level football. Transfer fees are ten times higher than they were a decade ago. We want television channels to reserve certain days for football, so there are more matches on one day and then football-free periods to renew viewers' appetites for the game. We have to take some fairly drastic action.' That action consisted of proposing a World Cup every two years, instead of four, and the launch of the World Club Championship.

It is easy to criticise international bureaucracies, such as the World Bank or the United Nations, with their limousines and huge, tax-free salaries. Typically a well-groomed spokesperson expresses his or her grave concern about the latest war, drought, famine, earthquake or epidemic before heading back to the air-conditioned office and a buffet lunch with aides. But, imperfect though they are, the world is a better place for having these organisations.

It is equally easy to denounce UEFA and FIFA. Under pressure from clubs, they are downgrading international matches and inventing new competitions to generate more money for clubs and themselves. But football is a unifying social force and an escape for youngsters from poverty in the developing world and it needs the expertise and support of international organisations. UEFA and FIFA, however, are running out of time. They must resist the insatiable demands of clubs for more competitions. They must ensure that the great international events, such as the European Championship and the World Cup, survive, not as optional add-ons to club events but as the supreme contests of football. In short, they must make it clear that football does not exist for the benefit of a few megarich clubs.

The FA has no such future and cannot continue in its current form. Apart from running the England teams – which could be done by a small committee of coaches and marketing experts – it has no function other than to exist and provide material for newspaper headlines. It should dissolve itself and become an umbrella for the Premier League, the Nationwide League, the non-league clubs and the amateurs. Of course, it will not do this; it will cling on, trying to find something to do. But one day football will decide that it has had enough. And the FA will vanish in a puff of self-importance.

Chapter Five

The Television Monster

Like most people in Britain I have a television set. I also have a video recorder, though I have never managed to record anything from the television. So on Saturday nights I often have to choose between *Match of the Day* on BBC1, Hollywood blockbusters on ITV, documentaries about Kosovo on BBC2, and studio debates on sex on Channel 4. I can also pick up Channel 5, but the picture is fuzzy. On Sunday afternoons I could watch Italian football on Channel 4 but the matches are so boring that I rarely bother.

Television companies say that people like me are the third millennium equivalents of nineteenth-century blacksmiths who assured each other that cars would never replace horses. Get with it, they urge, and embrace the exciting new world of football on our satellite, cable and digital channels. If you do not, you will be left with football highlights in between go-kart racing, tag-team wrestling and junior gymnastics. Occasionally you will be able to watch the finals of major competitions, such as the FA Cup, which the Government quaintly describes as events of such national importance that they must be shown on boring old terrestrial television but the broadcasting giants add that it won't be long before they buy these up, too, and if they can't get their hands on them they will invent other competitions for the major clubs and these historic competitions will become irrelevant.

To enjoy top-class football in the early twenty-first century requires technical expertise. You need a satellite dish, decoder box and a cable running into the street. Once this hardware has been installed you must be able to zap between channels, timing your run perfectly so that you do not sign up for the wrong match. This is tricky since there are so many channels it is easy to log on to the wrong game or the wrong sport. You also need money. You have to pay monthly subscriptions, although an increasing number of events are known as 'pay-per-view', which is telemogul-speak for extracting more money from customers. You might also want an interactive facility, so that you can change camera angles or track a player. And all this will cost more.

You must have lots of free time. Evenings and weekends should be spent interacting with Manchester United, Arsenal, Chelsea, Liverpool, Spurs, Barcelona, Inter Milan, Lazio, Marseilles, Vasco da Gama, São Paulo, River Plate, Boca Juniors and other giants of the world game as they battle for another title dreamt up by the television companies in association with the clubs and the game's governing bodies. In the future they will be joined by new clubs, which television's billions will fund, in the Middle East, Africa, the Far East and Australia. You will see more top-class football than any human being in history and you will not have to leave your home. You will not have to wrap up against the cold and the rain, travel to a ground, breathe fresh air or sit alongside real people as they chomp burgers. You will not have to watch journeymen players who have mortgages and drive battered cars; instead, you will be warm and cosy and will be guaranteed multimillionaire superstars.

This is an exaggeration, but not by much, of the future envisaged for us by television. Until the early 1990s televised football was a treat: *Match of the Day* on BBC on Saturday nights, regional games on ITV the following day. The FA Cup Final was broadcast on both channels; the World Cup and the European Championship were shown every four years; marriages foundered as husbands insisted that they could not go on holiday because these tournaments were too special to miss.

Computers, once a tool of the elite, have become the most potent force for change since the wheel. We live by cash points and swipe machines. Household appliances are tiny and multifunctional. Cars self-diagnose faults. Soon we will use our mobile phones to watch television, shop and surf the Internet. Millions own computers at home that are linked to the Internet and its limitless opportunities to learn, play, chat, buy and sell. Televisions, computers and mobile phones are becoming interchangeable.

Without this new technology football's revolution would not have happened. In February 2000 the future was foreshadowed as BSkyB and cable giant NTL scrapped with each other for a slice of Sports Internet, which *The Financial Times* described, in the jargon of this new age, as 'a sports web site and online betting company'. The *FT* announced that a tie up like this would allow 'programming content, of which sport is among the most valuable, to be delivered to consumers via the Internet on computer screens, mobile phones and televisions'. In layman's language this means that sport, especially football, will be inescapable; you will be able to watch Manchester United play Chelsea on your mobile phone while you sunbathe in Spain, assuming that you have subscribed to United's new pay-per-view digital-phone station, order Arsenal's new replica shirt for little Sam as you sit on the train, or experiment with Chelsea's super new digital instant-replay service, which will allow you to summon incidents from any Chelsea game from the past decade, while you wait for the waiter to take your order.

Sky and its competitors do not care what happens to the minnows of the lower leagues because this is about making money and it is too bad if the weak do not survive. Meanwhile, the football authorities insist that everything will be fine because, somehow, miraculously, television's money will filter down to the lower divisions.

Television sets in Britain used to be boxes which showed programmes broadcast by the BBC and ITV. In the 1980s satellite and cable arrived, offering the kind of choice that Americans had been enjoying for many years. But television remained a recreation not a lifestyle.

The new television companies, led by Rupert Murdoch's BSkyB, created in 1990 when Murdoch's Sky gobbled up the ailing British Satellite Broadcasting, had to sell dishes and decoder boxes to a public which doubted that it needed more than BBC and ITV. Sky had channels dedicated to films, shopping, repeats of classics, news and documentaries but none grabbed Mr and Mrs Average. Sky could not understand what was wrong because this was how it was in the States. But America is another country. It is so vast that national television does not exist; the three major networks, CBS, ABC and NBC, feed their output to hundreds of local stations.

American football has been shaped by television; games are punctuated by huddles and the exchange of offences and defences so that there is room for commercial breaks. Americans also need statistics to enjoy a sport. Football there is built around yards won and interceptions made, making cricket, the English sport which is most obsessed with statistics, seem innumerate. Baseball, damned unfairly by the British as rounders played by podgy men in tight trousers wearing silly hats, is also about 'stats'. Basketball is a freak show played by giants. Americans are consumers and are proud of it. Sport in the States is about excess – huge players earning piles of money – and glamour; it is Hollywood with sweat. American football teams regularly shift homes – one season a team is based in Chicago, the next it is in Florida, with a new name, because someone thinks that it will be more profitable. This is like relocating Manchester United to Brighton and renaming it Brighton United.

The moguls of satellite television assumed that the British wanted the same twenty-four-hour television service as the Americans, but they were wrong. The British read newspapers – national, regional and local – and listened to the radio in the morning. Homes traditionally had one television set, in the living room, which was only turned on at night; Americans, however, belonged to the first audio visual culture, where most homes had two, or more, sets. Satellite television decided, therefore, that it needed a must-see element which would hook the C/D social classes before addressing better educated and more prosperous people. And that hook was football.

Many sports had been transformed by television before the arrival of satellite dishes and smart cards. A few decades ago motor racing was practised by badly paid daredevils, watched by a few thousand cognoscenti, who could explain exactly why Jim Clark cornered more effectively than Graham Hill. Then Bernie Ecclestone took control. He realised that motor racing could be turned into an international spectacle. The cars would be billboards for motor and tyre manufacturers and would be plastered with the logos of multinationals, including tobacco companies, pariahs in the civilised world and desperate to be associated with an activity which was fast, glamorous and healthy. By the end of the century the average Grand Prix was watched by 350 million people and, according to a recent book, *The National Wealth*, sucked in about one third of the money spent globally by companies on sports sponsorship. The star drivers earned tens of millions a year; the also-rans, who made up the majority of the Grand Prix travelling circus, are paid the equivalent of a decent lottery win every year just for taking part.

In the 1970s the Olympics were turned into the biggest sports show in the world by television. But athletics, the sport which was the linchpin of the Games, did not prosper independently. In the 1980s ITV bought the rights to five years of major athletics in the country for £10.5 million, five times more than the BBC had previously been paying. Sponsors were also keen and pumped in an additional £5 million. But it did not work. Television had assumed that, because viewers were glued to their sets for the 100 metres or 1500 metres Olympic finals, they would be equally enthusiastic about any races involving the same runners. They were not; people watched the Olympics because they were a unique combination of nationalism and individualism, of medal tables, showing where Britain stood in the world, and of instant heroes, such as the marathon runner who had given up his job as a road sweeper in Bolton to train and who won a silver, not because they were interested in the events. In the mid-1990s ITV abandoned athletics, which Channel 4 picked up for a cut-price £4 million over four years.

Other sports fared worse. Show jumping, which had been a recreation for toffs, was taken up by television because it was cheap to film – a few cameras could track a horse around the arena; because drama was guaranteed – someone always fell off; and because riders were articulate and often attractive – there were many young men and women who looked dashing in their breeches and boots. But television grew bored with horses jumping over fences. Snooker had been played by pasty-faced, unemployed men in smoky clubs until television realised its potential: it also was cheap to film and the game had a satisfying ebb and flow; the calm of safety shots was followed by the explosion as a player smacked balls into pockets. In the 1980s snooker seemed unstoppable and its stars, like Steve Davis, became multimillionaire celebrities. In 1985, 18.5 million people watched Davis lose to Dennis Taylor in a world final. But, again, television lost interest.

Boxing, on the other hand, was a major sport until the new television stations acquired it. Instead of fights being shown live on BBC or ITV they were sold to satellite or cable broadcasters, who paid millions for the exclusive rights in the hope that boxing fans would subscribe to their services. This was excellent news for promoters and boxers who became rich but disastrous in the long term because boxing, traditionally a working-class sport, could only be watched by a minority.

Other major sports, however, realised that terrestrial stations ensured a mass audience. But they also saw that satellite television had an insatiable appetite for sport and would pay for second rights to major events and first rights to those which the BBC or ITV did not want. ('Rights' is the most heavily used word in the sale of sport to television. If a television company has first rights to an event it can show it live – or, failing that, before anyone else;

companies with second rights have to wait before they can broadcast it.) Tennis insisted that Wimbledon and other Grand Slams had to be shown by the BBC. Major golf tournaments could be watched using a decoder-free television. Rugby union internationals were free, providing that you had a licence. Horse racing knew that it depended on betting, and remained the staple of afternoon television. Cricket had tried for many years to become viewer-friendly by inventing the one-day game but decided it had to do more in the 1990s. Games were played under floodlights by players in Technicolor pyjamas and their appeals and banter were picked up by microphones in the field while tiny cameras buried in the stumps allowed viewers to share the batsman's experience. But cricket could not compete with football; the entire sport in England was worth about £75 million a year in the late 1990s, compared with Manchester United's annual turnover of £88 million.

The viewing figures confirm the gulf between football and the rest. In 1966, 32 million people watched England win the World Cup at Wembley. In 1986, 24 million people watched England play Argentina in the World Cup; a decade later the same number watched the two sides play in France in the World Cup. With the exception of motor racing and golf, other sports lost heavily in a more competitive market: snooker misplaced 10 million viewers in a decade, athletics 2 million, tennis 9 million, cricket 500,000, rugby 2 million and winter sports 4 million. But more people than ever were playing football regularly – up from 3 million in 1989 to 6 million in 1999, an increase of 100 per cent; the nearest challengers were tennis, up from 3 to 4 million, and rugby from 300,000 to 400,000, both equivalent to around 33 per cent.

Football has always dominated the world. Of the three major sports in the United States, two – football and basketball – cannot be played by normal people. Other sports – cricket, rugby, tennis, golf, athletics – have limited appeal. Some, like golf and tennis, are based on wealth; others, such as cricket, are culturally distinctive.

But football is the global game. It can be played by anyone, anywhere. One hundred and seventy-four countries tried to qualify for the 1998 World Cup in France. A fifth of the world's population, 1.2 billion people, played the game every day in 1998. Everyone, apart from Americans, loves football.

Television, however, was ambivalent about football in Britain until the 1990 World Cup in Italy. The previous tournament had a global audience of just under 15 billion people and generated about £0.5 billion from the sale of television rights; the competition in Italy was watched by 25 billion people and cost television almost £1 billion. The tournament in 1994 in the United States was watched by 30 billion people and generated £1.2 billion from television; over 35 billion tuned into the competition in France in 1998. The World Cup in England was worth just £2 million; the 1996 European Championship in England in 1996 generated £150 million, only a third of which came from ticket sales.

In 1987 British Satellite Broadcasting had tried to save itself by doubling the £3 million paid by the BBC and ITV for rights to top-class football. They rebuffed BSB easily by offering £11 million a year, which would be dismissed as a bad joke today. In 1992, however, everything was different. The top clubs had formed the Premier League and were determined to exploit the rivalry between the terrestrial and satellite broadcasters. Sky decided that football would be its saviour and made an unprecedented offer of £304 million over four years, with the BBC as junior partner: £214 million of this was for the rights to Premiership games in England, the rest for matches abroad. This was only the start. In 1996 Sky paid £670 million over four years for rights to sixty Premiership games per season; for £73 million the BBC would be able to show highlights on Saturday. But the next deal, due to begin in 2001, will dwarf this. Thanks to football Sky had almost 8 million customers by the end of 1999 and was expanding into digital technology; to keep existing customers and lure new ones it would pay as much as it had to to retain the rights to the Premiership.

There were other lucrative television deals for the major clubs in the late 1990s. Sky digital, an offshoot of Sky, snapped up the UEFA Cup. ITV bought Wednesday night matches in the Champions' League for a reported £165 million over four years as well as rights to the FA Cup and Worthington Cup. ONdigital, owned by Carlton and Granada, which relied mostly on Sky for its football, broke off and bought an exclusive chunk of Tuesday night matches in the Champions' League, which Sky did not have, for £80 million over four years.

The average viewer could not understand this network of interlocking deals. Many people thought that their aerial, satellite dish and digital decoding box meant that they would be able to watch the cream of games; but often they could not. For example, in September 1999 only 250,000 people in Britain saw Manchester United play Croatia Zagreb and Arsenal against Fiorentina in the Champions' League because ONdigital owned the rights and Sky's digital box was not compatible with ONdigital's. Nor could they pop out to the local pub to watch these games because ONdigital did not have the same commercial licence as Sky and its games could not be shown publicly. The press and the fans protested but ONdigital was unmoved: 'Once viewers realise that ONdigital is the only place where they can watch every Champions' League match they will be encouraged to subscribe. We know that it will take a little time but we are confident that it will happen,' said a spokesman.

In December 1999 Deloitte and Touche, the London accountants who monitor football's finances, produced a football rich list. This showed that Manchester United were the wealthiest club in the world, with an annual turnover of £87.87 million, though these results were based on the 1997–8 season, when United did not win anything, rather than 1998–9 when they won the Premiership, the FA Cup and the Champions' League. (It was expected that United would report a turnover for that season of £111 million.) Seven other English clubs – but only one Scottish – were in the world top twenty: Newcastle were fifth with an annual turnover of £49.2

million, Chelsea ninth at £47.5 million and Liverpool tenth at £45.5. Arsenal did respectably, thirteenth at £40.39 million. Rangers turned over £32.52 million, Aston Villa and Spurs reported just over £31 million each, putting them at seventeenth and eighteenth, and Leeds £28.26 million, giving them twentieth place. Celtic, West Ham, Everton and Derby turned over £20 million or more.

Nine clubs turned over between £15 and £20 million: Wimbledon, Blackburn, Leicester, Sunderland, Middlesbrough, Coventry, Sheffield Wednesday, Bolton and Manchester City. Four turned over between £10 and £13 million: Wolves, Barnsley, Southampton and Nottingham Forest. Twelve clubs, including once mighty teams which had slipped out of the top division and were hoping to spend their way back, turned over between £5 and £10 million. These were solid results, though it was clear that these clubs would never have the money to buy the players or stadia which would enable them to become elite members of the Premiership.

But many clubs were clinging to solvency. Seven turned over less than £1 million: Colchester, Shrewsbury, Scarborough, Darlington, Rochdale, Cambridge and Swansea. Eighteen limped along on less than £2 million. Thirteen reported turnovers of less than £3 million, including clubs with glorious histories such as Stanley Matthews' Blackpool, runners-up in the First Division in 1955–6. A few teams, including Brighton, did not cooperate with Deloitte and Touche, presumably because they were too embarrassed to disclose their pathetic revenues.

It is obvious that the adage, the rich get richer while the poor get poorer, applies conclusively to football. The turnover in the Premiership had risen by 350 per cent since its inception in 1992; from then until the end of the 1997–8 season it was estimated that its total turnover had been £2.15 billion. In 1997–8 turnover rose by 23 per cent from the previous season to £569 million. But profits did not reflect this. To survive in this division clubs had to spend more, on upgrading their stadia, on transfers and players' wages. As a consequence overall profits only rose from £86.6 million to around £100 million.

Players' wages were the major expense. Premiership clubs paid almost £200 million to players, a rise of 40 per cent on the previous year. On average over half a club's turnover went to players, though some were handing over virtually their entire income, which was financial suicide. The average Premiership player earned £190,000 a year but some were paid much more. In February 2000 it was estimated that sixty players in the Premiership earned £1 million or more a year from their clubs.

Wages in the First Division averaged between £75,000 and £100,000, far more than most clubs could afford. But they dipped dramatically after that: £40,000 a year in the Second Division and £25,000 to £30,000 in the Third. Although the average Third Division player made less in a year than a Premiership star earned in a week, the small clubs did not have the revenue to justify even these modest salaries. Forty-eight of the seventy-two clubs recorded a loss in 1997–8. Some, such as Swindon and Crystal Palace, behaved like gamblers on a losing streak and tried to spend their way out of trouble, with predictably disastrous results. Manchester United earned about £1.4 million on an average match day in the 1997–8 season, which was roughly what a Third Division club made during the entire year. The Premiership made a pre-tax profit before tax of £20 million, compared with the Nationwide's loss of £52.95 million.

First Division clubs had a turnover of £175 million, of which 68 per cent went to players. In Division Two the figures were £66 million and 84 per cent, and in the Third Division an ominous £26 million and 97 per cent. Thus, the smaller the club the greater the percentage of revenue went to players. During their Treble-winning year, Manchester United probably turned over more than the clubs of the Second and Third Divisions put together.

Every survey produces the same result: a growing gulf between the top clubs and the rest. The smaller clubs are spending more than they make and, barring a miracle – such as the arrival of a megarich patron or an outbreak of philanthropy by the elite – are destined for oblivion. The elite of the Premiership receive more from the broadcasters because they are more popular. They spend this money on new, exciting players, which makes them even more attractive. And so it goes on.

In the 1998–9 season Premiership clubs received £148.2 million from Sky and the BBC. But there was a huge gap between the Premier elite and the rest. The twenty clubs each received a flat fee of £3.52 million but, on top of that, using a formula based on appearances on television and their final positions in the league, Manchester United and Arsenal were paid over £6 million, which meant that each club made over £10 million that year from television. Then came Chelsea with £9.89 million, Leeds with £9.09 million, Aston Villa on £8.89 million and Liverpool on £8.75 million. Spurs, Derby, West Ham and Middlesbrough made between £7 and £8 million. Everton, Newcastle, Coventry, Leicester and Sheffield Wednesday received £6 million or more. The trailing pack – Blackburn, Southampton, Charlton, Nottingham Forest and Wimbledon – made £5 million or less.

Recently relegated clubs such as Barnsley, Bolton and Crystal Palace were each paid £1.73 million to try and boost their chances of returning to the top division. But this money would only buy the right leg of a moderate striker and, anyway, would only be paid in the two seasons following relegation.

The seventy-two clubs of the Nationwide League, meanwhile, are paupers. A league spokesman said that these clubs received £25 million a year from television, though most of that went to the First Division members. He calculated that the twenty clubs of the Premiership received seven times more money from television than those of the Nationwide.

The Premier League assures everyone that its clubs are worried about the chasm between the Premiership and the rest. Hence, over four years £50 million of television money has gone to lower grades of football, including £5 million to the Football League and £7.5 million to the Professional Footballers' Association. The

Premiership has also promised to donate 5 per cent of the next television deal to deserving causes. But these are gestures, not solutions. Meanwhile, the Premiership clubs squabble about what really matters to them: how to make money. They cannot decide what to do about those matches that are not selected by the broadcasters. The elite, such as Manchester United, Arsenal and Chelsea, know that they can make tens of millions of pounds by transmitting every match, either through an established company, such as Sky, or by setting up their own stations. But the smaller clubs fear that this will be catastrophic because they will not be able to attract similar audiences.

Football has never been democratic. There have always been a few successful clubs, pursued by dozens that dream of glory and many more that are simply grateful to survive. Carlisle and Brighton were in the Third Division in the late 1990s but had been in the First Division in the 1970s and 1980s. Blackpool, Burnley, Preston and Oldham of the Second Division also had memories of greatness. Most of the First Division of 1999 were once in the old First Division or the Premier League. Movement between the First Division and the Premiership is guaranteed by the annual relegation and promotion of three clubs but most promoted teams return immediately to the First Division because they do not have the resources to match even the also-rans of this top division. There are exceptions – such as Middlesbrough and Newcastle United – but it requires extremely wealthy patrons (such as Middleborough's Steve Gibson or Newcastle's Sir John Hall) who will spend tens of millions of pounds on players to prosper. Nottingham Forest, First Division champions in 1997–8, were relegated immediately back to the First. Blackburn, another club with a proud history, had boomed in the early 1990s, courtesy of a multimillionaire benefactor called Jack Walker, a local man who had made his fortune in the steel industry, and had won the Premiership in 1995. But Walker's money was not enough; unlike clubs based on the urban sprawls of the North East, Blackburn was a small, rundown town and could not sustain a Premiership team. In February 2000 they were a mid-table First Division team again and seemed likely to remain one.

Another local-boy-made-good, Jack Hayward, a tax exile in the Bahamas, has failed more spectacularly. Hayward has lived abroad since the 1950s and became one of the richest men in the world by developing Freeport, a tax-free industrial zone on the island of Grand Bahama; but he never forgot Wolves, the club he watched as a young boy. Wolves were league champions three times in the 1950s and are one of the most famous names in football but they decayed rapidly in the 1980s, like the factories where their supporters had once worked. In May, 1991 Hayward bought the club for £22 million and over the next decade spent tens of millions developing the famous old stadium, Molyneux, and on players. But it has not worked. Hayward can afford to buy good players but cannot persuade the best to come to Wolves. His money has provided a foundation but the catch-22 is that real success can only be achieved by promotion.

The best hope for clubs like Wolves is that the Premiership will recruit them into a Premier Division Two. In autumn 1999 it was suggested that the elite of the Premiership wanted to reduce the number of league matches because of mounting commitments abroad. The Premiership would be cut from twenty to sixteen and twelve teams from the First Division would be recruited to join the four ex-Premiership clubs into a sub-Premiership. It was not clear, however, whether clubs would be promoted and relegated to and from this new division; if not, it would signal the end for the other fifty-six clubs because football needs dreams.

Clubs can also pray that a major company will invest in them. Leading the charge are television and 'leisure' companies, such as BSkyB, NTL and Granada. But, again, money attracts money. NTL have grabbed a slice of Newcastle and Aston Villa and Granada have moved into Liverpool, while BSkyB is busily buying shares in clubs everywhere – Leeds, Manchester City, Sunderland, Manchester United and Chelsea – because they believe that clubs like these, with massive followings, will eventually launch their own pay-per-view stations, which will show every first team game.

Clubs such as Manchester United, Newcastle, Arsenal, Liverpool and Chelsea have millions of fans in Britain and abroad, few of whom have ever seen their team in the flesh. Analysts believe that these clubs can earn up to £100 million every season from their own stations, in addition to their existing income.

Many fans are offended by these developments. They complain that football is being reduced to a handful of giants which will become multinational businesses, not clubs rooted in a community. The two Premier Leagues will consist of an elite and no-hopers. The latter will exist only to provide opposition for the giants, for whom domestic competition will be an inconvenience, to be fitted in between lucrative European and intercontinental fixtures. And the fifty-six English league clubs who are not members of the two Premier divisions will fade into part-time oblivion, or worse.

When people feel that they have been cheated, they need to find villains. There are two: Rupert Murdoch, the most powerful media tycoon in the world, who controls BSkyB, News International and much else besides, and Manchester United, especially Martin Edwards, its chairman and chief executive. This is unfair. Murdoch is ruthless but he is a builder, not a destroyer, and is only exploiting new technology and shifts in social behaviour. He has offered large amounts of money to football but it could have refused him; it is not his fault that the sport is run by short-sighted men only interested in increasing the money coming into the game. United are despised for being the best and for making it clear that they know this. But other clubs, including bankrupt and homeless Brighton, are just as keen on success; they are simply not as good at achieving it. Edwards, however, deserves to be criticised; not for being so interested in money, which most people are, but for lacking the intelligence to disguise this.

The true villain is football itself – governing bodies, clubs,

broadcasters and even fans – who claim to want the unpredictabil-
ity of the good old days but who actually love it when their clubs
become so powerful that domestic matches are seen as a second-
rate grind. It requires foresight – the growing inequalities within
the game will destroy it – and courage – today's profits will be
wiped out if wage inflation is not curbed – to admit the scale of the
crisis, let alone find a solution. But football does not possess these
qualities.

It must also be remembered that football fans are illogical. The
yobs of every club always hate their local rivals. Status is
irrelevant: fans from Newcastle, Middlesbrough and Sunderland
loathe each other but so do the lunatic followers of Plymouth,
Exeter and Torquay. Feuds develop for reasons that only a
sociologist can explain; hence, Manchester United and Liverpool
yobs always try to tear each other apart but United's meetings with
Leeds do not generate the same passions. Ask United and
Liverpool fans about this and they talk in images: Manchester is
flash and cocky; Liverpool is thick and poor.

My friend Mick Brown, the journalist, exemplifies this. Apart
from his club, Crystal Palace, whom he loves but also despises, he
does not mind Brighton, because they are so useless. He quite likes
Leeds, although he hates Lee Bowyer, one of Leeds' young stars.
Chelsea are 'ponces'. West Ham are okay, because the manager,
Harry Redknapp, is 'good fun'. He also dislikes Wolves, for no
reason, but has a soft spot for Coventry, though he does not care
for the manager, Gordon Strachan. He hates Blackburn and
Manchester City. But Grimsby are good: 'It's great when they
come to Palace. We chant, "You are supposed, you are supposed
to, you are supposed to smell of fish." And they sing back, "We are
supposed to smell, we are supposed, we are supposed to smell of
fish." ' He adds, 'But everyone hates Manchester United, don't
they? Why? Because they are Manchester United.'

The division of the country between supporters of Manchester
United and everyone else is a recent phenomenon. The Munich air
crash of 1958 provoked enormous sympathy, even in Liverpool.

During the 1960s, as Busby strove to win the European Cup as a memorial to those who had died at Munich, the country willed him to success and joined in his celebration when United beat Benfica 4-1 at Wembley in 1968. Apart from hardcore bigots, everyone admired Bobby Chalton and adored George Best, the Irish genius whose life – 'I spent a lot of money on birds, booze and gambling – the rest I just frittered away' – anticipated the philosophy of the glossy lads' magazines of the late 1990s.

United were also popular during the 1980s, as the club tried to recover the glory of the Busby era. The club tried flamboyant managers, such as Tommy Docherty and Ron Atkinson; both men brought flair on the pitch but embarrassment off it and had to go. United tried serious men, such as Dave Sexton, but they were too dull.

In November 1986 they hired a Scot called Alex Ferguson, who had been a humble striker in Scottish football but who had emerged as a formidable manager at Aberdeen. For four years nothing happened and United seemed doomed to remain another once-great club, which had faded like the industrial working class on whom its fortunes had been founded. Then United beat Crystal Palace in the FA Cup Final replay after the first game had been drawn 3-3. No one took much notice but it marked the start of the revolution which saw United transformed into a multinational business, like Coca-Cola or Nike.

In June 1991 the club floated on the Stock Exchange, which enabled the public and investors to buy shares in it. Previous football flotations had not gone well: the first club to do so, Millwall, ended up in receivership and the second, Spurs, had to be saved by that traditional figure, the millionaire, in the shape of Alan Sugar. The City was not impressed by United that June and less than half the available shares were taken up.

Martin Edwards had inherited the club from his father, Louis, a meat merchant. Although he had always insisted that United was in his blood, this did not stop him trying to sell his stake in 1989 for £10 million. But, fortunately for Edwards and for United, the deal collapsed. While Edwards presided over the modernisation of the club off the field, Ferguson performed miracles on it and the team dominated the 1990s, collecting five Premiership titles, four FA Cups, a European Cup Winners' Cup and, best of all, the Champions' League in 1999.

Although Edwards and Ferguson did not like each other – Edwards thought that Ferguson was surly and disrespectful; Ferguson seethed that Edwards would not pay him as much as other, less successful managers – they were an irresistible team.

Glory on the pitch was exploited ruthlessly off it. The club opened three shops at the ground – the Superstore, the Megastore and the Matchday Store – where it sold replica kits and assorted club memorabilia. It set up a web site on the Internet which was a miniature supermarket for loyalists in Britain and overseas. While other clubs spent fortunes on the wrong foreign players, Ferguson invested wisely abroad and blended imports with youngsters who had been nurtured in United's youth team.

In September, 1998 BSkyB moved. Sensing that the Premier League giants would set up their own pay-per-view stations, thus undermining Sky's appeal, Rupert Murdoch offered to buy United for £623.4 million. Edwards, who would have made £85 million from the sale, and the directors, with the exception of Greg Dyke, a multimillionaire television executive who later became Director-General of the BBC, were in favour. But the fans were not. Marshalled by a tenacious journalist called Michael Crick, author of a hard-hitting biography of the novelist and failed politician, Jeffrey Archer, the fans triumphed. The Monopolies and Mergers Commission ruled that the sale could not go ahead because it was against the public interest, was anti-competitive to other broadcasters and a threat to the health of football generally.

The fans celebrated this as a victory for Joe Public. 'Our feeling is one of absolute euphoria. We have shown that United must remain independent,' said Andy Walsh, of the Independent Manchester United Supporters' Association. Another anti-Murdoch fan said, 'This has drawn the line in the sand. All those media conglomerates who have been planning to take over clubs will have to go back to the drawing board.'

The fans turned on Edwards and pointed out that, while he was refusing pay demands from star players and the manager, his own remuneration had shot up from £120,000 in 1991 to £593,000 in 1998. Their disgust at Edwards was understandable – he only seemed to be interested in his own bank balance, which was already a row of noughts – but their joy at rebuffing Murdoch was curious. The club was a publicly quoted business, legally obliged to make as much money as possible for shareholders; it was a company, without moral purpose.

The manager, players and fans did not see it like this. They used the ancient clichés of the game – about the next match being vital, about taking nothing for granted, about bouncing back from defeat – but United the Company was constantly expanding. It developed its financial institutions, such as a United savings account, built a new training complex and signed deals with a club in South Africa to monitor local talent who might make the grade in England.

In the summer of 1999 the club visited Shanghai and Hong Kong, not because Ferguson thought that his lads needed the practice but because the marketing experts thought that the region offered exciting opportunities. The club was already selling its merchandise in Singapore, Malaysia, Brunei, Thailand and Indonesia through agents, and planned to open stores and 'Red Cafés', where locals could watch United's matches, throughout the Middle and Far East. To journalists and fans who believed that this was too mercenary, Edwards replied that football had changed. It was a world game and United needed the financial muscle to compete. Italian and Spanish clubs had their own pay-per-view stations which produced annual incomes of £30 million or more so United had to make money by selling its image or it would fall behind. When Manchester United took part in the World Club Championships in January 2000, United the plc saw its future in global events like these, playing against teams from every continent, rather than in FA Cup games against Third Division nobodies.

But few clubs prospered like United. Although only one, Maidstone, folded in the 1990s many are hanging on, like chronically sick patients who refuse to accept that it is more sensible to give up because life is so painful. Some, such as Gillingham and Bournemouth, have been rescued from bankruptcy by fans; others, like Southend, have sold their grounds to developers. Traditionally, small clubs had survived by selling their best young players to the major clubs but these transfers were increasingly rare by 2000, because of the influx of foreigners into the Premiership, and because managers of major clubs needed the instant allure of big-name signings to satisfy television, which, after all, was paying the bills.

Every day brought news of another club in crisis. In February 2000 it was Swindon's turn. In the early 1990s Swindon had been managed by Glenn Hoddle, but he departed for Chelsea and then England. Under John Gorman the club had one dreadful season in the Premiership in 1993–4 – they won five games and conceded a hundred goals, which is still a record. Steve McMahon, the former Liverpool midfielder, replaced Gorman but could not halt the decline and the club was relegated again in 1995. A year later he led them back to the First Division.

But the club was devastated by the cost of trying to regain its place amongst the elite and was broke by 2000. The chairman, Cliff Puffett, admitted that it had all been too much. After promotion to the First Division in 1996 he had been told by McMahon that he needed £3 million to take the club into the Premiership. 'We chased the dream. We budgeted for average crowds of 12,500, which would rake in £2.5 million, then £300,000 from the conference facilities at the ground, with some of the board ploughing in the difference. But then the ball hits the post, and stays out and the striker misses a sitter. Wins turn into draws and draws into defeats and the crowds aren't there,' he said.

It is a familiar pattern. A club believes that it has to spend to accumulate. It buys players whom it cannot afford, but they are not quite good enough. They are not promoted and the crowds dwindle. But the highly paid players remain. The club cannot sell them, because the Premier clubs do not want them and lower division sides cannot match their wages. So the debts mount, until there is nothing but red on bank statements.

Swindon will probably stagger on. Commercial logic suggests that clubs like this should become part-time or fold but there is still extraordinary sentiment about football; we are attached to the dozens of little clubs whom we know only through pools coupons. But sentiment does not pay bills and one day, perhaps this year, perhaps next, reality will have to be faced: without major reforms the small clubs will disappear.

Chapter Six
Home Talent

Early in February 2000, there was relief from the shocking story about a doctor called Harold Shipman who had just been sentenced to life imprisonment for murdering elderly patients: David Beckham, of Manchester United and England and husband of Victoria Adams, otherwise Posh Spice of the Spice Girls, might leave United.

While pundits speculated on Shipman and the nature of evil, football reporters were probing Beckham. Stories like these become true the moment that they are published; whatever the source of the Beckham report – a member of Posh's entourage advertising David's availability or a preemptive strike by United – it was indisputable that Beckham wanted more money than his captain, Roy Keane, who had just been given a contract worth £52,000 a week. It was also a fact that Mrs Beckham did not like Manchester or United's manager, Sir Alex Ferguson.

This was more than a story about a footballer; it was a drama about an attractive and wealthy couple who were living out the fantasies of many young Britons. The media was ambivalent about David and Posh; they did not *deserve* to be such stars but, on the other hand, they were a phenomenon which could not be ignored; and, like the late Diana, Princess of Wales, they sold newspapers. Middle-aged Middle England does not equate money and fame with success – nurses, teachers, police and fire officers and lifeboat crews perform unacknowledged, heroic deeds every day – but the young believe that success means multimillion pound houses, expensive cars and clothes, exotic holidays and invitations to parties which are reported in *Hello!* To this generation Beckham, 25, and Adams, 26, had made it.

It was reported that Beckham's 'advisers' had asked for £60,000 a week from United. The club would probably concede – knowing that Beckham would cost at least £20 million to replace on the pitch and that he generated millions off it as an icon – but the press thought that he might still leave Old Trafford. His wife felt that they would be happier in London or a chic European city, such as Milan, Barcelona or Rome. Manchester was provincial and Ferguson treated her husband as if he were a mere professional footballer. Ferguson was always warning Beckham about the dangers of distractions, such as modelling, being paid £1 million by magazines to be photographed in their lovely new home with their baby son, Brooklyn, going to film premieres and popping over to New York to shop. Posh thought that Ferguson was a dinosaur: David should be living in a metropolis where the public could adore them and where other important celebrities lived.

It was rumoured that Posh favoured Arsenal, a grand old club which had recently abandoned its policy of capping players' wages by offering £28,000 a week to a Nigerian striker Nwankwo Kanu. But she knew that David was worth three times that. Chelsea were vulgar and, anyway, had too many egotistical and handsome foreigners who would be jealous of David. Spurs were tight-fisted and were managed by George Graham, a puritanical, disciplinarian Scot like Sir Alex. West Ham were beneath him. If Arsenal did not table a suitable deal Posh would instruct David's advisers to open talks with European clubs who would be delighted to pay him properly, which meant more than £60,000 a week, plus perks.

It was thought that Arsenal would have to pay £40 million to United, a world-breaking sum which would be hard to refuse. If United blocked the deal and hung on to Beckham, he would be able to leave for nothing in two years when his contract expired. There was also the possibility that he would sulk and lose form or be injured; if that happened his value would plummet.

Although Arsenal were the thirteenth richest club in the world – with an annual turnover of £40.39 million – they could not raise £40 million, together with a contract which would pay Beckham a minimum of £3 million a year. Arsenal had banked £23 million from selling Nicolas Anelka, a talented but petulant French striker, to Real Madrid, but would still have to find another £20 million or so. It was suggested that this could be accomplished by inviting a television company to take shares in the club, which had happened at other Premiership and Nationwide clubs, but which Arsenal, proud of its independence, had always resisted.

The saga of Beckham and Posh sums up the new football. Money is the new god; the megastars appear in media rich lists, alongside Internet entrepreneurs, the landed aristocracy and the barons of television, and are paid hundreds of thousands of pounds by gossip magazines for exclusive access to their weddings, homes and christenings.

In football, as in life, only money matters. Beckham is an amiable young man from east London, the son of a gas fitter, who left school without passing any examinations and who would probably have become a tradesman, like his father, if he had not been blessed with sublime athletic ability.

A few days later Ferguson hit back. Beckham missed a training session in Manchester because Brooklyn was suffering from a cold at the couple's £2.5 million house in Hertfordshire. If the child had been seriously ill, Ferguson would certainly have been sympathetic – although he is a disciplinarian he is not a monster – but it was obvious to him, and his players, that Beckham had used his son as an excuse; training was now something to be fitted in alongside his other engagements, such as modelling and escorting his wife to fashion shows.

Before his marriage Beckham had been a model professional who spent hours practising free kicks and crosses; Ferguson was part-father, part-headmaster, part-boss to him, as all great managers are to their players. But now Beckham thought that he had outgrown Ferguson. He was a major 'personality' and should be treated with respect. Ferguson did not agree. Beckham was a fine footballer, not one of that band of 'celebrities' who were famous for being famous and who wasted their lives courting publicity and complaining about lack of privacy.

So he acted. He dropped Beckham from a vital match at Leeds to prove that no one is bigger than United. But Ferguson knew that ultimately he could not win. Before television's millions and the Bosman ruling players had been terrified of losing their place in the first team or being transferred but stars could now ignore their managers. If they were unhappy they could sulk; the club could either sell them or risk losing them for nothing when their contracts expired. Ferguson mumbled privately that he was relieved he was reaching the end of his management career; try as he did, it was becoming increasingly difficult to control players who did not appreciate that fame and wealth had to be earned.

There was an uneasy reconciliation after the Leeds match but no one believed that it was permanent. Beckham was a superb player, but he was not indispensable; he threatened the culture of hard work and selflessness which had brought United a string of trophies and, sooner or later, would have to go.

The transformation of professional footballers – from men who earned the same as miners and who travelled to games by bus to multimillionaire celebrities who always turn left when they board a plane – has taken a century.

In the early 1900s there was a maximum wage which decreed that a player could not earn more than £4 a week (worth about £200 in 2000, less than a general labourer picked up in 2000 for mixing concrete and smashing down walls). Transfer fees averaged £400 (about £20,000 in 2000). Players were bought and sold by clubs and, if they did not agree to this, could not play for anyone else. Attempts by the players to extract more money from clubs, and to abolish the transfer system which was sport's version of serfdom failed.

In the mid-1940s the maximum wage was £9 (about £200 in 2000). In 1947 Blackpool bought Stanley Matthews – the right winger who many believe to be the greatest player in the history of English football – from Stoke for £11,590 (about £250,000 – in 2000 a young Stanley Matthews would cost at least £30 million). Tom Finney, Matthews' rival for the title of the most accomplished English forward in history, had signed for Preston North End in 1937 when he was fifteen and had been paid £2.50 a week (£75 in 2000). In his career, interrupted of course by the war, he played four hundred and thirty-three matches for Preston and scored one hundred and eighty-seven goals. He was capped seventy-six times by England and scored thirty goals. He was Footballer of the Year in 1954 and again in 1957, and remained one of the biggest crowd pullers in the history of the game until he retired, a one-club man, in 1960. In the mid-1950s, at the height of his career, Finney was on £12 a week (£180 in 2000). He lived in Preston, took the bus to the games and was grateful to be paid to play a game he loved, in between earning an extra few bob as a plumber.

Late in 1999, then aged seventy-seven, Finney said,

I wouldn't swop places with today's players and they earn more in a week than we did in our whole careers. Whenever David Beckham goes anywhere with his wife, look at the commotion. It was never like that for us. We were allowed to live our lives. When we had a young family we'd go on holiday to Blackpool by bus.

I used to catch the train at Preston and meet Stan Matthews and Stan Mortenson [the legendary centre forward who played twenty-five times for England] of Blackpool when we made our own way to international matches. It was a totally different world.

Finney said that his wages had been good by contemporary standards – about twice the national average. He had also had a deal with a firm of boot makers in Kettering. To complete his financial portfolio, England had paid him £20 per match at the start of his career, which had risen to £50 by the time he retired.

Although Prestonians worshipped Finney the club never let him forget that he was a humble employee. In 1952 an Italian club offered him £120 a week to play for them (£2,000 in 2000), plus a villa and a car. 'The Preston chairman looked at me and said, "If tha' doesn't play for us, tha' doesn't play for anyone." That was it, end of story. There was nothing I could do. The contracts were totally in the clubs' favour.' Even if Preston had been willing to sell him to an English club Finney would not have been any better off, since he was earning the maximum wage in the 1950s.

By 1961 the maximum wage had soared to £20 during the season and £17 during the off-season (£260 and £220 respectively in 2000). That year Jimmy Hill, the chairman of the Professional Footballers' Association later to become the anti-hero of television punditry, and the PFA secretary, Cliff Lloyd, forced clubs to abandon the maximum wage. To the astonishment of the country it emerged that Johnny Haynes of Fulham would now receive £100 a week (about £1,300 in 2000). Two years later a court ruled in favour of George Eastham, whose club, Newcastle United, had tried to stop him moving to Arsenal. From then on a club would not be able to retain a player's registration after his contract had ended. The PFA were still not happy, however, and protested over the years that clubs behaved as if players were inanimate objects, to be retained or sold at will.

The clubs finally lost control when a Belgian player, Jean-Marc Bosman, incensed that his club, FC Liège, had refused to sell him to a French team for a reasonable price, asked the European Court of Justice to rule on the nature of the relationship between clubs and players. In 1995, five years after Bosman fell out with Liège, the court ruled in his favour. It said that the European Union was based on freedom of labour; hence, players over twenty-four years old could leave their clubs for nothing when their contracts expired.

*

In the mid-1960s the arrival of George Best of Manchester United heralded the era of the player as pop star and fashion icon, but Best's status owed more to his genius on the field and his flamboyance off it than to the size of his pay packet. In 1969 Best, who had, a year earlier, helped United win the European Cup, decided that it was time to move out of the room which he had rented in the council house of Mary Fullaway, a widow with two sons. She had been his surrogate mother since he had arrived in Manchester as a gawky fifteen year old from Belfast. Today's teenage superstars earn thousands of pounds a week, live in luxury houses and pop out to the local Porsche dealer on their eighteenth birthday but Best had been happy to share a room with other United hopefuls, and to travel to training by bus. Team-mates at United who lacked his charisma did not fare so well; a television documentary in 1999 revealed that some members of the team that won the FA Cup in 1963 were paid £30 a week (£360 in 2000).

The best insight into football in the years when Best dominated the back pages is *The Glory Game*, written by Hunter Davies, who was given unprecedented access to Spurs during the 1971–2 season. In the preface to the June 1990 edition of his book he wrote that, superficially, everything had moved on in the twenty years since publication, but added, 'The clothes, the money, the characters have all changed. But inside any professional club I suspect that things are very much the same. The tensions, the terrors, the tedium of training, the dramas of the dressing room, the problems of motivation, the clashing of personalities, are all very similar.'

By the time these words, written in June 1990, appeared in the bookshops they were already out of date. The World Cup in Italy that summer turned top players into celebrities. Two years later came the Premier League and satellite television's hundreds of millions and then, in 1995, Bosman.

Davies described how even players at Spurs, one of the richest and most successful clubs in the country in the 1970s, were permanently worried about losing their places in the team or being injured or transferred. At the root of this was money; they earned excellent wages, which allowed these working-class young men, most of whom had left school without any qualifications, to live like the middle classes. But players still had to find jobs when they retired. In the 1990s most players in the Premier League, and some in the First Division, did not endure the anguish described by Davies; they did not fear anyone or anything because they were rich long before their legs started to lose power.

The players who featured in the book are forgotten now. The stars were Martin Chivers, a hulking, moody centre forward, Alan Mullery, a hard-working wing back; Martin Peters, an elegant midfield player who had been a member of the World Cup winning team in 1966; Alan Gilzean, a Scottish forward of bewitching skill; and Pat Jennings, one of the finest goalkeepers in history who won one hundred and nineteen caps for Northern Ireland. In 2000 they would have been multimillionaires but in 1972 they were only comfortable, at least while they were playing for Spurs.

There were no Afro-Caribbeans or exotic foreigners at the club. Spurs players were white and working class. Their fathers were miners, machine operators, painters, bricklayers and so on. Most had left school at sixteen and had gone straight to a club, though a few had worked in menial jobs, such as portering, before becoming players.

Most were married, with young children, and lived on estates in the leafy suburbs of north London in houses costing about £20,000 (about £160,000 in 2000; this compares with the £500,000 that Beckham and Posh spent on their wedding). Some had business interests outside football, such as shares in sports shops or fish and chip shops, activities which would definitely not appeal to today's superstars. They drove family saloons, played golf and watched lots of television. Most only read the back pages of the tabloids, if they read a newspaper at all. Many holidayed in Britain and those who did venture abroad usually chose Spain.

All were worried about the future. Alan Mullery said, 'it was a big problem'. He did not know how he would find another job which would pay £5,000 a year (£35,000 in 2000). Another said that he would like to work in a holiday camp, organising 'the sports side . . .' Some hoped to survive by running shops or garages and others dreamt of becoming coaches. Most did not want to become managers; some because they were too modest, others because they thought that managing was an awful job. (In fact, many did become successful managers, notably Mullery, Joe Kinnear, Mike England, Steve Perryman, and Graeme Souness, a young reserve player at Tottenham in 1972.)

In 1972 an established member of the first team picked up between £80 and £100 a week, but bonuses could add several thousand pounds a year. Players in the top half of the First Division averaged around £7,000 a year (about £56,000 in 2000) and those in the bottom half about £3,500. Second Division players made about £2,500 (£20,000 in 2000) but Third and Fourth Division players had to survive on the wages of a 'semi-skilled factory worker'. The new star of that season was Ralph Coates, whom Spurs had bought from Burnley for £190,000. In 2000 Coates' agent would have ensured that his client wanted for nothing when he arrived in London but it was not like that in 1972. The club deposited poor Coates and his wife in a flat in north London which did not even have a telephone.

Major clubs today employ doctors, dieticians, physiotherapists, fitness specialists and physiologists to ensure the physical and mental well being of players but in 1972 Spurs made do with a seventy-year-old ex-player as a physiotherapist. He had a room full of equipment but was not sure how to use it and, anyway, thought that most injuries could be 'run off' since overcoming pain was all about character. Like most clubs, Spurs also pumped cortisone into injured players, which often caused serious problems in middle age since cortisone destroys soft tissue if it is used as an all-purpose painkiller. Football clubs were still run by men like Spurs manager Bill Nicholson, who hated long hair and who thought that the maximum wage had been a good thing because players could not afford to answer back. Players were treated as if they were idiots: Hunter Davies reported that the Spurs doctor always warned players at the beginning of a season about the dangers of extra-marital sex.

It was no better at other clubs. Tommy Smith joined Liverpool in 1959 at fifteen and became a vital member of Bill Shankly's unbeatable team of the 1970s. He played over six hundred games for the club from 1963 until 1978 but ended up broke and disabled in the late 1990s. Like many ex-professionals he is not impressed by the players of the 1990s. They are paid fortunes to play fewer games and are protected from the kind of tackling which had been routine in the 1970s. Smith concedes that players today might be faster and fitter – 'what with eating spaghetti and all that' compared with the 1970s diet of steak and chips and beer – but, on the other hand, they play on immaculate 'bowling greens' with balls which are 'balloons', unlike the mud heaps masquerading as pitches and the deadweight balls of the 1970s. No, Smith concludes, the players of his day would stuff the late 1990s generation if they were young again.

Peter Lorimer, a member of Don Revie's great Leeds United team of the 1970s, was paid about £300 a week before tax, 'even if we were really flying'. Lorimer, who ran a pub in Leeds after he retired, said, 'Nobody in my day retired on what they made out of football. Players now get a security which we never had and it makes it difficult for any manager to get discipline or loyalty.'

Not every player from the 1970s ended up like this. Many members of the Manchester United teams of the 1970s prospered after they retired. But this did not indicate that players then were better educated or more resourceful than their predecessors, only that this particular team possessed above average intelligence. Steve Coppell, a winger whose career was ended prematurely by injury, became an acclaimed manager. Martin Buchan, the United captain, became UK promotions manager for Puma after an unsuccessful stint as a lower division manager. Buchan said that he would have preferred to have been playing in 2000 – and getting rich – but was happy with his life. Others did equally as well. For example, the goalkeeper, Gary Bailey, became a television pundit in his native South Africa; Kevin Moran became an agent for the stars of 2000; and Joe Jordan, the gap-toothed, battering ram centre forward became a top-class television pundit.

But others fell apart after injury or age forced them out of football. Mickey Thomas, a winger, served nine months in prison in 1993 for handling counterfeit bank notes and greeted the new millennium in a council house in Wales. Thomas thought that it was unfair that a player like him, who used to mesmerise Old Trafford, should have ended up like this. 'When I joined United I got £18,000 as a signing on fee. I put that into a pension, which I live off now. At United I got £450 a week and on top of that I could get a win bonus of £750 a week, which was a lot of money for a boy from a poor background.' Paddy Roche, the reserve goalkeeper, was driving a van in Lancashire in 1999 and Jimmy Greenhoff, a midfielder who would have been worth several million pounds in 2000, ended up working for a wallpaper company. Tom Sloan, who was never a regular member of the United first team, became a plasterer in Northern Ireland. Arthur Albiston, a full back who played five hundred first team games in fourteen years at Old Trafford, also found it hard to cope with life after United. He said, 'I have no qualifications and football is all you've got.' Another full back, Mike Duxbury, said that he had tried to become a coach when he retired but 'nothing came of it'. He found a job teaching football at a school.

In the 1980s football was preparing for the boom of the next decade, though no one realised it at the time. The old managers, hard-faced disciplinarians like Nicholson, Shankly and Revie, were being replaced by sleek ex-players who wore expensive suits and haircuts. Unlike the men who ran football in the 1970s, and who had principles, however primitive, the new breed did not believe in anything but themselves, which meant that they would embrace new ideas – such as signing black or foreign players – if it was good for them.

Hunter Davies recorded many of these developments, albeit in more restrained terms, in 1985 in a new introduction to a reprint of *The Glory Game*. He reported that Spurs had become a slick business. The old physiotherapist had gone; players' meals were planned by a dietician and their minds were monitored by a psychologist. There were only thirty-one full-time players, compared with forty-one in 1972, because higher wages had brought smaller squads, but the administrative staff had almost doubled. The players earned on average about £40,000 a year, which was good but not spectacular (about £75,000 in 2000). The first team squad was broader, both socially and racially. A few players were middle class and could have gone to university; there were several black players and an Argentine, Ossie Ardiles. But players were still mainly white and working class and their aspirations were as limited as those of the Spurs players of the early 1970s: they hoped, somehow, to make a living after they retired.

In the late 1990s the Premier League successors to these players had very different experiences. They were paid huge amounts of money, which meant, in the pap-speak of their agents, that they were 'financially secure' for life, unless they were stupid enough to blow their money on women, gambling or booze.

Their relationship with the media was complex. Many journalists thought that their salaries were an affront to fans and would eventually destroy the sport; others were simply jealous that thick young men who used the 'f' word as a substitute for thought earned more in a week than people like them, with university degrees, made in a year. But the new football was essential to the success of a newspaper or a television station.

There were hundreds of stories about David Beckham as his romance and then marriage to Posh elevated him to the position of super-celebrity. Apart from the daily bulletins on his fitness and relations with his manager, he often featured in the news pages. After being caught speeding and being banned from driving, a court let him off because he pleaded that he had been trying to evade the paparazzi. Posh did not help; she babbled constantly, as if her brain was not connected to her larynx. She said that she did not understand football, that baby Brooklyn had cried at a match, that she could not bear to be separated from David and, once, with truly stunning stupidity, announced that he liked putting on her underwear. It was impossible to escape them. They stared out from magazine covers, wrapped around each other in self-adoring poses, their taut bodies glistening. Even *Vanity Fair*, the American magazine which regards most British celebrities as also-rans, stuck them on the cover of its British edition. But, with so much space to fill, the press also had to interview other stars of the Premier League regularly. Most just gibbered clichés about the pressures of earning £40,000 a week. Occasionally there were genuine stories, which revealed the unchanging brutishness of football. In February 1999, during a match at Stamford Bridge, Robbie Fowler, the £35,000-a-week Liverpool forward who looked and sounded more stupid than he was, bent over invitingly as Graeme Le Saux, Chelsea's full back, was preparing to take a free kick. Le Saux snapped because he knew that Fowler was goading him about his rumoured homosexuality.

It emerged that Le Saux, an intelligent, middle-class lad from Jersey who was not, and had never been, gay, had endured years of abuse from his fellow professionals who thought that anyone who read the *Guardian*, liked museums and art galleries and once went on holiday with a male friend instead of with the obligatory blonde 'model', had to be gay. Fowler's taunts during the match – 'poof' and 'faggot' – culminated with the obscene invitation to Le Saux.

None of this was welcomed by football, which was marketing itself to the middle classes as glitzy and stylish; the sport did not want its new fans to know that many of the players thought that it was 'poofy' to read serious newspapers or enjoy art.

Like all top players, Fowler traded on his image – advertisers and sponsors do not, after all, want to be associated with bigots – and tried to repair the damage the following summer by appearing on a current affairs programme on ITV. It was painful to watch

Fowler, a pleasant but inarticulate young man, being questioned about his behaviour by a journalist, as if he were an Oxbridge-educated politician instead of a working-class boy who was paid a fortune to kick a ball.

But at least Fowler had the courage to appear on television and the humility to admit that he had been an idiot. Other young millionaires were not so polite. But journalists were awestruck and sycophantic when they should have dismissed such players as ill-mannered and ungrateful. For example, the Saturday *Times* magazine once profiled Andy Cole, Manchester United's striker. *The Times* drooled over Cole, analysing his grunts and snorts as if he were a philosopher.

But, to be fair, Cole knew what he was and did not care. Yes, he said, it was unjust that he was paid so much when people like his sister could not find a job despite having a degree. But that was not his fault. Life was about making money and he was doing better than most, including the bloke from *The Times* who was interviewing him.

Steve McManaman, the flop-haired, languid winger who always promised to be great at Liverpool but never quite made it, joined Real Madrid in summer 1999 on a free transfer. He was also a favourite with the press because he was paid so much – estimates varied from £55,000 to £65,000 a week – and because he spoke in sentences rather than grunts punctuated by obscenities.

The press were also intrigued by the very young stars. Top of the profile list was Michael Owen of Liverpool, who had become famous in the World Cup in France in 1998 when he was still a teenager. Unfortunately, Owen is quiet, polite and thoroughly decent and is only interesting because he is so wealthy. (Liverpool paid him a basic salary of £32,000 a week. He also received millions more from sponsors.) *The Sunday Times* magazine once asked him to describe his day for its series 'A Life in the Day'; this was memorable only because of its triteness. He got up, trained, ate, played other games, such as golf, and went to bed. He was totally, miraculously, unconcerned about the world.

Home Talent

For some young millionaires life is more exciting. In March 2000 two Leeds United players, Lee Bowyer and Jonathan Woodgate, were charged with allegedly causing grievous bodily harm after an incident outside a nightclub which left a young Asian student badly injured. Leeds emphasised that they were innocent until proven guilty but added that, if they were convicted, they would not play again for the club. This was common sense rather than morality: if found guilty they were likely to face prison sentences, and, more important, no club could survive in an ethnically diverse area like West Yorkshire if it employed players convicted of a racist attack. But, whatever the outcome of the trial, the case raised again the question: was it wise to pay young men so much money? Woodgate and Bowyer were paid £15,000 to £18,000 a week respectively and drove matching blue BMWs. Together they were worth about £20 million on the transfer market.

Leeds United had one of the worst images in the country in the 1970s. The team was successful but brutal and Leeds fans were racist and violent. The club worked hard in the 1990s to change this. The racist chanting which greeted visiting black players was curbed and hooligans were banned. Under its young manager, David O'Leary, once an elegant centre back for Arsenal, the team had been rebuilt around a core of homegrown youngsters. But, like all managers in the Premiership, O'Leary had a problem: he had to control young men of limited intelligence who had already made more money than the average fan earned in a lifetime. If he dumped his best players, the club would drift down the league and he would be sacked. This was amoral but it was fact: football clubs had always been concerned with money, not the rights and wrongs of issues, and were certainly not going to change now, when success meant millions of pounds.

The strain of celebrity often proved too much for older players. Tony Adams, the Arsenal and England centre back, described in his autobiography, *Addicted*, how he had fought against alcoholism. Paul Merson, who had made his name at Arsenal before moving to Middlesbrough and then Aston Villa, also talked bravely about his addictions to booze and gambling. But others, such as Stan Collymore, were lost souls; Collymore should have been one of the country's top strikers but his career disintegrated in a haze of self-pity. But, thanks to Bosman, Collymore was still being paid £20,000 a week as he shuttled between clinics and clubs.

The most dramatic example of a player being ruined by money and fame was Paul Gascoigne, whose tears during the World Cup semi-final against West Germany in Italy in July 1990 had helped to redefine football. By 2000 Gascoigne, now almost thirty-three, was a pathetic figure. Two years earlier Middlesbrough's manager, Bryan Robson, the former Manchester United and England player, had paid Glasgow Rangers £3.45 million for Gascoigne, in the belief that he could extract one final flourish from the player. He was wrong.

Both men were Geordies and both enjoyed a drink. But that was all they had in common. Robson had been a magnificent player; to natural energy, aggression and guts he had added tactical awareness and skill. Gascoigne, in contrast, had started with everything – speed, balance, strength and dazzling skill – but had wasted it. Great players of the past, such as George Best, had succumbed to the temptations of drink and women but Gascoigne was the first of the modern superstars to crash. He was an ordinary, working-class lad, cheerful, boisterous and often plain silly, who could not handle money and fame. Successive managers in London, Rome and Glasgow tried to control him but they failed, probably because it did not really matter to them how he lived off the pitch as long as he still performed on it. So they tolerated his boozing with his pals from the North-East and his jaunts to London's West End with 'celebrities' – and then sold him. As he grew older he was injured more often because he was never fit and, depressed that his body was failing, drank even more. He married but that ended in accusations of wife-battering, and divorce. Middlesbrough dispatched him to clinics to dry him out but it was too late.

Home Talent

Robson was not the only manager to find himself with a player who was earning a fortune for doing nothing. The Bosman ruling had encouraged clubs to offer long-term contracts to players. This was good business if the players continued to perform but a disaster if they did not. At Newcastle, for example, twelve players who had been signed by one manager, Kenny Dalglish, found that his successor, Ruud Gullit, did not rate them. So the twelve, whose weekly wages came to about £100,000, ended up as the highest paid fitness fanatics in the country. It was difficult to sell them to other Premiership clubs because they were not performing and the players would not move to smaller clubs because that would have meant taking a pay cut.

A few players became 'issues'. Alan Shearer was constantly profiled because he was so rich (it was estimated that he was worth £17.5 million in 1999) and because his feud with Ruud Gullit ended with Gullit's resignation as manager of Newcastle.

The managers of the smaller Premiership clubs occasionally snapped as wages soared, pushing them closer to bankruptcy. On the eve of his sixtieth birthday, Derby's manager, Jim Smith gave an extraordinary interview to the *Daily Mirror*:

People like me can't scare players into action any more. I used to deal with players who kept whippets as a hobby – now they own bloody racehorses instead. Many of them are not in soccer because they love it but because they love the money.

When I shout at them, when I rant and rave, I am wasting my breath. I can see a lot of them thinking: 'What the hell is this old fart on about?' It makes me sad to think players care so little. It is almost as if football is an inconvenience which threatens to interfere with their champagne lifestyles.

In a way I feel sorry for present-day players. They are missing out on the camaraderie we used to have in football. They don't seem to be enjoying themselves very much, despite their big houses, flash cars and the rest of the trappings that loads of cash can bring. It's sad. They are losing so much laughter along the way and you wonder whether the young lads of today understand what fun this great game can be and what memories it can create for future years.

Steve Coppell, the manager of Crystal Palace, a club teetering on the edge of bankruptcy, agreed. He told *The Sunday Times*:

There's a great American saying, 'Why bother getting out of bed when you're wearing silk pyjamas?' And I think that this applies to some young footballers. It's not a problem at Palace because we haven't got the money but elsewhere a lot of youngsters are earning huge amounts of money before they're the finished article. Some of them undoubtedly find it hard to motivate themselves. People are often motivated by knowing that success will bring financial rewards but, if the money is there too early, their potential can go unfilled.

Niall Quinn, Sunderland's striker who wrote columns for quality newspapers, was also worried: 'Players with six cars worry me. I fear that some young players are losing touch with reality. Because there is so much money in the game it is only right that we get our proper share but I would like to see young players on big five-year contracts being paid the money over a ten or even fifteen year period so that they didn't have so much in their pockets.'

Ex-players did not approve either. Geoff Hurst is the only player to score a hat trick in a World Cup Final. For the game against West Germany in 1966 he received a match fee of £60. He told a newspaper that strikers in 2000 no longer pushed themselves because they were on huge, long-term contracts.

Forwards have no incentive to risk getting hurt in the penalty boxes like we did because we were always trying to impress our club bosses and, of course, the England manager. Our contracts were never more than eighteen months so we had to get the goals to be re-signed. Getting into the England team was not just a matter of pride for us, it was also a way to enhance our value as players.

Now, with long contracts and massive wages, players don't need to be internationals to be rich. With the top stars on £40,000 a week even ordinary players are getting £25,000 a week. Where is the incentive to strive to get better. It's human nature to sit back and enjoy the comfort zone of your fat contract.

Hurst pointed to the goalscoring rates of his contemporaries: players such as Clive Allen, Ian Rush and Ron Davies had all scored over forty goals in a season, as he had done twice. He pointed out that today's forwards rarely hit as many, although the kind of tackling which was common in Hurst's era had been outlawed. 'It's very sad for the fans because goals are what the game is about and they're getting short-changed by players they're helping to make millionaires. These players live like film stars, own fabulous homes and drive magnificent cars without having to get hurt as we used to.'

This is a subjective judgement but it is undeniable that, despite complaining that they are exhausted, the Premier League millionaires play less than their predecessors. In the 1965–6 season Bobby Moore played seventy-two matches, including six European ties and sixteen internationals; in 1979–80 Brian Talbot of Arsenal played seventy games; and in 1983–4 Sammy Lee of Liverpool turned out in seventy-two matches and helped win his club the First Division title, the League Cup and the European Cup. But David Beckham only managed fifty-three games for Manchester United in 1998–9, when they won the Premiership, the FA Cup and the Champions' League, and five games for England. Other millionaire stars with successful clubs were even less active: Frank Leboeuf of Chelsea played forty-five times and Lee Dixon of Arsenal forty-six times.

Top clubs, involved in lengthy cup runs here and abroad, replied that they were playing more games than in the past but that was a feeble argument because they had such large squads. In 2000 Manchester United could choose from half a dozen international strikers; when Arsenal won the League and the FA Cup in 1971 they played sixty-four matches and used just sixteen players.

There is another football, though, where players earning £30,000 or £40,000 a year are watched by a few thousand spectators. This is the world of the Second and Third Divisions, where clubs survive on hope, stubbornness and creative accountancy. Here players worry about the mortgage, about being injured, about being dropped and about the future.

Some clubs in the First Division believe that they will return to the cash-strewn Premiership from which they were relegated; others are sure that, if they splash out a few more million on players, they will be promoted. But few in the lower divisions have any such faith in future glory. It was possible once for a club to shoot up the divisions but that was before the Premiership and satellite television's millions. Today it is hard to see how any small team will be able to outwit the mini-giants of the First Division without a stupendously rich patron, who would have to spend millions on players without any guarantee of success.

Once, promising young players from the lower divisions would be bought regularly by the major clubs and patiently nurtured. But big clubs today require instant success, which means buying established players from each other or from abroad. As a result small English clubs become even more desperate for money and ask too much for their best young players, which frightens off potential buyers.

There are 2,500 professional footballers in the four divisions and the few full-time non-league teams. There are around five hundred in the Premiership; the remaining 2,000 or so work in the Nationwide League, averaging between twenty-two and twenty-five per club. The major clubs of the First Division pay well – they have Premiership quality squads – but wages fall sharply in the Second and Third Divisions. Fifty thousand pounds a year is an excellent wage here but many players receive £25,000 or less. In 2000 such salaries were respectable enough if you were a young doctor or accountant, but players on salaries like these would have to start again when they retired, mostly without a single qualification.

Ironically, as money pours into the Premiership, more players in the lower divisions are losing their jobs. The PFA estimated that five hundred players were looking for new clubs during the summer of 1999. A few had deliberately let their contracts expire, confident that they would be signed by another club on better terms, but many more had been sacked. There were a number of reasons for this, all stemming from the boom in the Premiership. The invasion by foreign players had pushed British players down to First Division clubs. They demanded Premiership salaries, which meant that fringe players had to be sacked. They moved down, squeezing the old and the less talented out of the Nationwide League.

Graham Taylor chief executive of the PFA, summed it up for the *Guardian*: 'The lower league clubs can't afford long-term contracts. Clubs are more willing to release players because they have a wider net to choose from. Premiership players out of contract don't usually have a problem getting fixed up with a club. If you're at the top of the tree you have a chance of picking up a branch a bit lower down. But when you are at the bottom it's different. Many of these players end up becoming semi-professionals or find another career.'

Many of these players had spent their entire careers in the anonymity of the lower divisions but the most poignant cases involved men who had once been at the top. They had begun their careers in youth teams alongside players who had become millionaires but now they were broke and unemployed. Perhaps they had lacked that fraction of pace which separated the stars from also-rans; perhaps they had suffered an injury at a crucial moment or perhaps booze, women or gambling had prevented the promise of youth from maturing.

Scott Patterson began his career at Liverpool, with players like Robbie Fowler and Jamie Redknapp. But in summer 1999, aged twenty-seven, he was looking for work. After Liverpool he had moved to Bristol City and then to Carlisle, in the Third Division. Then Carlisle released him. He said that his agent had approached ten clubs but only one, in the Third Division, expressed interest with the offer of a trial, which was hardly a morale booster to a player who could have been starring for Liverpool. Another twenty-seven year old, Sean McAuley, who had begun his career at Manchester United, was also searching for a new club after Scunthorpe let him go. He had written to forty clubs but none had offered him a contract. McAuley sensed that things were changing for players like him: 'Football has given me a good life but I don't know how long it will last. I can't retire on my earnings and it's getting harder to find work. Many players in the Third Division could be forced out of the professional game.'

It has always been grim for the journeymen. In 1976, Eamon Dunphy, a skilful Irish midfield player, in his late twenties, published his diary of 'four eventful months' in the 1973–4 season at Millwall, then a mid-table Second Division club. It was called *Only A Game?* and was a marvellous book which captured the fear and frustration of players like Dunphy who knew, in their hearts, that they deserved more. Dunphy, who later became a successful journalist, talked constantly about money: 'We had children, mortgages, cars that didn't start, wives that bitched, overdrafts and gardens that needed tending.' All footballers, he said, are supremely selfish because all that matters is playing well in the first team; if it is a choice between that, and the team playing well without you, then every player would prefer the team to struggle, though the fans would be shocked to hear it.

Twenty years later another journeyman professional updated Dunphy's account of life outside the top league. Garry Nelson was a striker in his early thirties clinging on at Charlton Athletic, a once-mighty club which dreamt of a return to the top division. The book, *Left Foot Forward*, was less poetic than Dunphy's but was more gripping because of the chasm which had by that time opened between the Premiership and the rest; in Dunphy's day there was a gap between the First Division stars and humbler pros but it was bridgeable; but by the mid-1990s Premiership players inhabited a different universe.

Nelson was as worried as Dunphy about money, as fearful of injury, as puzzled by loss of form and as frightened about the future, but there was a new element: the wealth of top-class players. Nelson admitted that he was jealous but also thought that the imbalance in the sport – between clubs turning over tens of millions and those that could not afford to buy players proper meals when they were playing away – was dangerous. Players like Alan Shearer, then with Blackburn, had cost so much that he had to be turned into a superstar. Nelson wrote, 'The press/publicity machine has to be geared up to get the last pound of spin-off financial return on his career . . . The people in Burnley and Bolton will be drawn in. Their impoverished local teams will lack glamour . . . The man who once would have gone to watch a dozen live games a season will now buy a satellite dish . . . And, by and large, he will see better games.'

Nelson also anticipated the impact of Bosman:

The smaller clubs would almost certainly be reduced to 'part-timer' status, or propagating talent for later harvesting, act very much as nursery clubs for big boys. You would just have to ask yourself how much would Andy Cole have received if he had been available on a free [transfer] instead of tagged by Newcastle at £7,000,000 [when he was sold to Manchester United]. The wealthy, arguably power-mad Premier clubs, will cream off the pick of the crop and monopolise the five-star players. They in turn will receive rewards and contracts rivalling the wildest dreams of avarice.

Nelson was right. But in 2000 there were signs that football realised that the old recruitment system – when scouts from the major clubs scoured the country for promising boys – was both inefficient and bad public relations. Talented boys often escaped the net, ended up at small clubs and had to be bought for inflated fees later. The system also attracted criticism from the media: the majority of apprentices were never offered contracts as professionals and staggered off tearfully into the world without any qualifications. So clubs set up 'academies' for would-be professionals. Football was central to the curriculum but coaches emphasised to the boys that few would be good enough to earn a living from the game. So they had to study and, if they did not, they would be thrown out.

This would not change the basic truths – that most boys who wanted to become professional footballers were working class and unable or unwilling to work for exams – but it was a start. And if it meant that one lad – who had just been told by the manager, 'sorry, son, we're letting you go' – had a future, then it was worth it.

The world is unfair. Posh Spice is a multimillionaire who spends more on a pair of shoes than a nurse in a casualty ward earns in a week. A spiv trader in the City picks up £500,000 after gambling on the shares of a new Internet company; an ex-Page 3 pin-up makes £40,000 for hosting a television quiz show. Premiership footballers are paid £50,000 a week even though they are no better than their predecessors, who earned £20. But that is capitalism and, until someone invents an economic system which is both just and free, it is the best we have. Under Communism star players were equally privileged; they had their own flats, Western cars and clothes and access to hard currency which made them as distant to their fellow citizens as today's Premiership players are to the average fan.

Economics, not morality, will determine what happens to the Premiership's millionaires. If football ceases to be fashionable, clubs will chop wages. Meanwhile, the sport must try to make these players less offensive. In the United States it is common for clubs to demand that their players behave properly; if they do not, they are fired. Companies in the States are also more wary than their British and European counterparts about endorsing players who booze, womanise, gamble or take drugs. Of course there are problems. An English player fired by a club for, say, beating up his wife would probably sue his club for unfair dismissal. But football has a duty to force its superstars to recognise that they are role models in a society where the young only respect money.

Chapter Seven

The Foreign Legion

The television crew arrive at the new £20 million training complex near Heathrow Airport, protected by a high fence, topped by barbed wire and scanned by video cameras. They show their BBC identity cards to the guard. He checks on his clipboard that they are expected and waves them through. They park their minibus alongside the Ferraris, Porsches and BMWs and unload the lights and cameras and the blue and white board – proclaiming that this is the BBC's *Saturday Football Special* – which will be the backcloth to their conversation with Jean Kauffmann, the Frenchman whom Chelsea have just acquired for nothing after his contract expired at Juventus.

One of the club's new public relations team, established on the advice of a director who was formerly a spin doctor to blue chip companies, escorts the crew and the reporter, Bob Walsh, a former Arsenal player who was capped twice for England in the early 1980s, to the interview suite. While the camerman, soundman and lighting technician fuss over their equipment, Walsh runs through his questions.

Down the corridor the first team squad is emerging from the showers after the final training session before flying to Cheshire, where they will rest in readiness for Sunday's match with Manchester United at Old Trafford. They are joint leaders of the Premier League. The game is all-ticket, as United's home games always are, and will be watched by 68,000 people, a record for the league, because the final tier of the new stand has been completed. It will be televised live on Sky digital, with interactive options available, at a price. Apart from Kauffmann, who is certain to start, Chelsea will probably field two Italians, a Romanian, a Czech, a Spaniard, a Croat, a Belgian and a Turk. There are only two Britons, though one is a Scot. The solitary local boy is the right back, who comes from a west London council estate and who signed for the club as a schoolboy. The likely substitutes include a French striker and an Australian goalkeeper.

In the dressing room players ignore the club rule that English must be spoken. An Italian is on his mobile phone complaining to his agent in Rome about the flat that Chelsea have rented for him in Kensington; it only has three bedrooms, compared with the four in the flat in the same block occupied by his Romanian colleague. The Croat is also talking on his mobile, urging his friend from Zagreb, who plays for Real Madrid, to come to London because the money and the women are unbelievable. The two Frenchmen are planning to set up a company to renovate houses on the Côte d'Azur.

Kauffman towels himself, blow-dries his hair, which has earned him £500,000 a year endorsing a shampoo which he never uses, and puts on his £1,500 suit. This is another nice little earner: he receives ten suits a year free from a Parisian designer, who also pays him £500,000 to advertise them. He leaves his boots – for which he is paid £1 million a year to wear by the manufacturer – to be cleaned by the staff. (The younger players, who used to be called apprentices, no longer have to perform such menial tasks.)

Kauffman was born in Marseilles. His father owned a small bar and drank so heavily that he died when Kauffman was eight. His mother took over the bar and tried to ensure that her three sons and one daughter had the education to equip them for success in life. One son became a doctor, another, Emile, became Jean's agent after training as a lawyer, and the daughter married a millionaire property developer. But Jean was always destined to become a professional footballer. He was not a good pupil, though he had a quick mind; he loved football and knew that he was exceptionally gifted. He also knew that he could earn more in a year as a top player than his teachers, who scowled when he said that he had not done his homework, made in a lifetime.

He is twenty-eight and is one of the most feared strikers in the world. He made his debut for Marseilles when he was seventeen and played for France two years later. Now he has thirty-two caps and eleven goals and would have had more if he had not told the manager that he was an idiot. After three seasons in the Marseilles first team, one French League title and a loser's medal in a European competition, the name of which he can never remember, he was sold to Barcelona for £4 million and a weekly salary of £12,000 after tax. Spain had been fine. Barcelona won the Spanish League twice, which the fans expected, but failed in Europe, which the fans could not accept. So he decided it was time to move. His wife, Marie-Claire, a former model in Paris who had given up work when the first of their two children was born, agreed.

Emile touted him around Europe's top clubs. Bayern Munich wanted him but he did not fancy Germany. Liverpool were also interested but there was no way that he was taking his family to a dirty, wet city in the north of England. He chose AC Milan. He was out of contract at Barcelona so, thanks to the Bosman ruling, the club could not demand a transfer fee. That was great because AC Milan could afford to treble his salary. There were the usual perks: a web of bonuses, a percentage of profits from the club's merchandising of his image, free villa, a club car (a top-of-the-range Ferrari), unlimited use of two mobile phones for himself and his wife and two flights a month by private jet to Paris, for meetings with Emile and his accountant.

Milan had been good. He picked up languages easily and within six months had added Italian to his Spanish and the English he had learned in Spain because he figured that it would be useful one day. Then Milan sacked the manager and he was sold to Juventus for £9 million. That was fine, too, but he became bored and decided to move when his contract ended. Juventus tried to persuade him to sign again but he refused. The club tried to sell him. He refused again because he would be a free agent soon, which meant an even better deal.

He told Emile to fix him up in London. Emile e-mailed Chelsea and Arsenal – he did not bother with Spurs, who were tight-fisted, or West Ham, who didn't have the money. The e-mail had been designed by a Parisian company and was as slick as a pop video: Kauffman scoring a goal for Marseilles; Kauffman in action for Barcelona against Real Madrid; Kauffman flying through Lazio's defence; Kauffman's personal trainer describing the player's physical attributes – speed, stamina, agility, extraordinary peripheral vision – and Kauffman talking, in English, about his boyhood dream of playing for Chelsea and for Arsenal. (He recorded these twice, of course.) Next, Emile leaked the news to a French news agency run by a friend that Kauffman was unsettled in Italy and that Manchester United were interested.

Arsenal and Chelsea bit immediately. Arsenal's package was excellent but Chelsea's was better: £50,000 a week after tax as a basic salary, bonuses, linked to appearances, goals and so on, and a generous slice of the profits from merchandising. The club agreed to pay £15,000 a month for an apartment, to pay for his two boys to go to a French prep school in Knightsbridge and for twice-weekly flights to Paris for his wife, who had opened a modelling agency there. Emile also demanded improvements on the 'add-ons' which Kauffman enjoyed in Italy.

The three-year deal was worth a minimum of £2.5 million a year after tax but if things went well he would make more. By the end of the contract his accountant calculated that he would have a net worth of £21 million, consisting of properties in Spain, Italy and France, restaurants in Paris, Rome and Barcelona, his vineyard in Provence and the third share in the Serie B club in Turin, his share portfolio and his antiques and art collection, which his wife had built up. He could also take a pension of £100,000 a year when he was thirty-five, but that was peanuts.

Kauffman walks into the interview room and shakes hands with Walsh and the film crew. Chelsea have given him a summary of

Walsh's career (a decent striker for ten years at Arsenal in the days before players made real money) because reporters are flattered if you know who they are. Kauffman says that he has always admired Walsh's contribution to Arsenal's League-winning team of 1982 and Walsh smiles, although he knows that this is bullshit. They sit down and the soundman pins the microphone to Kauffman's lapel.

The truth never emerges. Kauffman is a professional footballer who does his best when he is playing because that is his job. But he cannot say this because fans expect him to pledge undying loyalty to the club; last week it was Juventus, now it is Chelsea. So he delivers the obligatory platitudes in fluent but charmingly accented English. Chelsea are a great club. They have wonderful players. He has always wanted to play for them. The Premier League is the ultimate challenge for any player. Team spirit is great. Foreign players can learn from British players and vice versa. He hopes to fight his way back into the French national team but his first priority is to play well for Chelsea. Italy was terrific but the football here is more open, which suits a striker like him, and the people in London will give him more space than fans in Italy, who were always bothering him. His family will be arriving soon and will love the city.

Then they move to the technicalities. Will he play as a front man or will he prefer to lie in the hole behind the strikers? What does he think of the fact that most of the team are foreigners? Isn't that bad for the game in England because local players are not getting a chance? Do the fans care about this? What does he think of Manchester United? Are they vulnerable at the back? And so on. Kauffman is open, amusing and modest. After half an hour Walsh thanks him and says it was really great.

Kauffman drives to the penthouse overlooking Stamford Bridge which Chelsea have given him while his wife looks for a permanent home, changes into another suit and leaves for a late lunch in Knightsbridge with the sports editor of the *Independent*, who wants him to write a weekly column. The money – £250 per column – will just about cover the price of a decent lunch but it will be fun to write and it will be good for his image. After that he will have a sauna and massage at the club because he feels stiff. Then he will have a light dinner of pasta and salad at the restaurant by Stamford Bridge with the manager, who is an Italian and a former team-mate at Barcelona.

Next week will be frantic. He has to film a shampoo commercial. He is starting to take Japanese lessons because he plans to end his playing career in Japan, where they pay millions for European stars like him. *Paris-Match* want to spend a day with him. The *Evening Standard*'s star interviewer wants to talk to him for at least two hours. His personal fitness adviser is arriving from Marseilles to check that Chelsea's training routines suit him. And there is a mid-week league match at home to Spurs.

Jean Kauffman does not exist and this interview did not take place. He is a composite, based on the tens of dozens of top foreign players who have swarmed into the Premiership in the past five years. They have come for the money; a decade ago they would have stayed in Italy, Spain or Germany but since the mid-1990s Premiership clubs have paid staggering wages and, since players are mercenaries who want to make as much as possible in their short careers, they come to England.

Chelsea have not paid anyone £50,000 a week after tax yet, but when Roy Keane asked for that figure (before tax), and threatened to leave the club if he did not receive it, Manchester United did their sums and paid up. Keane could have left for nothing, since his contract only had a few months to run, and it would have cost at least £15 million to buy a replacement, who would have demanded at least £30,000 a week. So the club reckoned that they were saving money by surrendering to Keane. These negotiations were followed with interest by players and their agents.

The smaller Premiership clubs might protest poverty when their star players ask for parity with Keane but Chelsea would not be able to argue that credibly. The club's wage bill rose by 81 per cent in the 1998–9 season, according to Deloitte and Touche. The top earners at Chelsea that season were foreigners: Marcel Desailly, the Ghanaian-born Frenchman, was on £35,000 a week; player-manager Gianluca Vialli was on £30,000; Pierluigi Casiraghi of Italy was on £28,000; and Frank Leboeuf from France received £25,000. Finally, there was an Englishman, Dennis Wise, the little midfield player with a cherubic smile and a ferocious temper on £22,000, along with Roberto di Matteo and Gianfranco Zola, both from Italy.

Kauffman's perks are also fictional, but the foreign stars of the Premiership enjoy benefits like these. An estate agent in London told me recently that Chelsea had asked him to find a flat costing up to £3,000 a week for a foreign player. He said that the club would pay the rent.

There are elements of the fictional Kauffman in many of the Premierships' star foreigners. Like him they look after their bodies and their wealth. Unlike English players of the past – and some today – they do not spend afternoons playing snooker before getting drunk and brawling in nightclubs. David Ginola of Spurs is multilingual and articulate – he has addressed the Oxford Union and was a pundit for the BBC during the 1998 World Cup – and advertises shampoo and cars on television. Frank Leboeuf writes a column for *The Times* and shops at London's most expensive stores with his attractive wife. Gianluca Vialli lives in a flat in one of London's most exclusive squares. Vialli also reads books, which would have identified him as a freak a few years ago when a handful of players, such as Trevor Brooking, who became footballers rather than undergraduates, were talked about with a mixture of awe and loathing, as if having a functioning brain was a betrayal of their fellow pros.

The best of the foreigners have brought class to the Premiership on and off the field. They come from countries where footballers are idolised but, in return, are expected to show respect to clubs and fans. British players have tended to be mumbling yobs and these elegant, thoughtful foreigners seem more like film stars than footballers.

But the fascination with these foreigners also shows that the English feel inferior; these players *seem* more interesting because they wear designer suits and come from Rome, Paris, Barcelona, Rio de Janeiro and Buenos Aires, which older fans only know from films. Ginola and Zola evoke images of sunshine, pavement cafés, open-topped sports cars, hotels overlooking still mountain lakes; everything, in fact, that the old Britain was not.

There is another factor: the glorification of money. During the 1980s Margaret Thatcher, the Prime Minister whose name became a description for a lifestyle based on self-interest, preached that money was the barometer of success; this seeped into the national psyche so that, by the late 1990s, the Labour Party was as keen on personal wealth as the Conservatives. Hence, foreign players who came to England for the money were admired by the Thatcher generation, though neither they nor the fans dared to put it as bluntly as that.

No one doubts that the foreigners have raised standards. The Europeans and South Americans are more agile and skilful. The Africans, too, have become favourites; they have limitless energy and enthusiasm – and a flair which was last seen in the era of George Best.

The Scandinavians bring decency and common sense. In *Staying Up*, Rick Gekoski noted that Coventry's Scandinavians were quieter, brighter and altogether more rounded human beings than British players. There are many reasons for this. Scandinavia is classless, or rather, uniformly middle class. Footballers in Scandinavia usually leave school at seventeen, with qualifications. Many begin as part-timers so they develop business interests, unlike young English players, who only have to think about the next game.

In the first seven years of the Premiership the number of foreigners rose from eleven to around two hundred, an increase of 1,800 per cent. In the 1996–7 season there were thirty-four overseas players in the division; the next season there were one hundred and thirty-four and the season after that one hundred and sixty-six. By early 1999 Chelsea led with fifteen players from the European Union and two from outside it; next came Arsenal, with fourteen from the EU; Liverpool, Newcastle, Sheffield Wednesday and Spurs had ten each, with six non-EU players between them; Leeds had nine; and Manchester United and Southampton eight from the EU. The smaller clubs, such as Wimbledon and Charlton, could only afford one EU player each but, interestingly, Aston Villa, one of the giants of the league, in terms of history and potential if not performance, only had two Europeans, Everton, another faded titan, had just three.

Fifty-five countries were represented amongst the twenty Premier League clubs and the seventy-two in the Nationwide League. It is possible to discern a pattern in these purchases. The elite of the Premier League can afford the very best. It is easier for a London club to attract a star from abroad because foreigners want to live in London. Clubs like Liverpool, Manchester United and Newcastle have to work hard to sign players used to cities like Rome, Milan, Amsterdam and Barcelona but they offer such huge salaries that many are persuaded. The also-rans of the Premier League have to make do with lesser or more temperamental players. The entire league, however, sweeps the world constantly, looking for bargains in the former Warsaw Pact countries and the former Soviet Union, in Africa, the Far East and the Caribbean and the smaller countries of Central and South America.

Europe remains the biggest source of players for all clubs. Decent players can be picked up for a few hundred thousand pounds from former Warsaw Pact countries and the fragments of the old Soviet Union, far cheaper than the equivalent talent costs in Britain. Non-EU players require a work permit, which they are granted if they are current internationals; that is not usually a problem because players who are ordinary by European standards are often valued members of footballing Third World national squads. St Lucia's Earl Jean plays for Plymouth; St Vincent's Rodney Jack for Crewe; and Australia's Andy Bernal for Reading.

The seventy-two Nationwide clubs are as keen as the Premier

League giants to sign foreigners, but do not possess networks of scouts and contacts abroad, so they rely on tip-offs and luck. The wages they offer, between £30,000 and £50,000 a year, are tempting to players in, say, Africa; the only problem is finding players who are not good enough to interest the Premiership clubs. Hence, the Nationwide clubs had only one hundred and fourteen foreigners between them at the start of the 1999–2000 season.

Jean-Marc Bosman was responsible for this; he completed the transformation of footballers from the badly paid serfs of the 1950s to men who could make millions from their talents.

Despite his limited abilities as a player Bosman is assured of a place in the history of the game. In 1988 he had joined FC Liège on a two-year contract. When it ended the club offered him another contract, at 60 per cent less money. Bosman refused to sign and the French club Dunkerque offered to buy him for about £125,000. But Liège wanted twice that amount. There was stalemate. Bosman would not re-sign for Liège and the club would not sell him, which meant that he was unable to earn his living. Bosman might have been an ordinary player but he was a remarkable individual; most players would have shrugged and tried to squeeze a few more pounds out of their club but Bosman knew that this was wrong and appealed to the European courts. It did not do him any good personally. He had drifted out of the game by the late 1990s and was so pressed for money that he asked his fellow professionals, who had become rich through him, for modest donations; disgracefully, none was interested.

The court's verdict in 1995, that Liège's action had been illegal because it amounted to 'a restraint of trade', changed the landscape of football. Players whose contracts had ended could now move, without transfer fees, between EU member states. Next, the court decreed that UEFA's limit of three foreign nationals – and two 'assimilated' foreigners – per team was illegal; from now on Chelsea, Manchester United, Roma or Barcelona could field eleven foreigners if they chose.

The likely repercussions were immediately obvious. Players

whose contracts had ended could move for nothing. Agents would demand huge salaries for their free transfer clients, which the clubs would have to pay. Next, clubs would try to tie star players to long contracts, which would also inflate wages. The lifting of restrictions on the number of foreigners in a team would lead inevitably to the richest clubs hiring the best talent, even if that produced teams composed of imports.

All sports depend on competition; there has to be rough equality between teams or the fans will lose interest. They will not pay to watch games where results are a foregone conclusion, because one team is stuffed with internationals and the other is composed of second-rate cloggers. In the United States the major sports have established systems to ensure that teams' fortunes can rise and fall by capping wage bills and giving the weaker teams the first choice of the most promising college players of each year.

European Union law, however, makes it impossible for football to impose similar safeguards to prevent a handful of clubs in each country monopolising the best talent and creating miniature domestic super-leagues. FIFA and UEFA say that they would like to introduce rules to halt this development – for example, by limiting the number of foreigners a club can field – but Brussels has said many times that the community will not tolerate any such restrictions. So football is helpless.

The statistics show what has happened. In the 1995–6 season Premiership clubs spent £28.5 million on foreign players, a quarter of their total outlay on all players. In the following seasons they spent 68.6 million, £84.1 million and £75.7 million respectively.

Liverpool bought eight players for £25 million for the 1999–2000 season. Seven came from abroad – from the Czech Republic, Finland, Guinea, Holland and Switzerland. Other Premiership clubs also shopped abroad because the Nationwide clubs were asking too much for their players and, in any case, the fans and television were more excited by a towering centre half from Africa than a young Geordie hulk from the Third Division. Thus, of the £125 million which the top clubs spent during summer 1999, only £1.4 million went to the Second and Third Divisions; put another way, the Premiership clubs spent £60 million in the summer of 1999 on players but £42 million of that went abroad. This was disastrous for the small clubs, who had survived in the past by selling their best young players to the giants. It is a vicious circle: the more desperate the small clubs become the more they ask for their young stars. Danny Mills of Charlton, a promising full back, cost Leeds £4 million, £1 million more than Chelsea paid for the brilliant French midfielder Didier Deschamps. Leeds also paid £4.5 million to Chelsea for Michael Duberry, a competent centre back who was certainly not in the same class as Jaap Stam, whom Manchester United bought from PSV Eindhoven for just over £10 million.

In summer 1999 only six players moved up from the Nationwide to the Premiership and two of these came from clubs that had just been relegated, which meant that, effectively, only four players had graduated to the top division. Young English players complained that they were being squeezed out by foreigners. Chelsea's and Arsenal's youngsters were especially unhappy as their managers, Gianluca Vialli and Arsène Wenger, went on regular spending sprees overseas. These youngsters conceded that they had learned from the foreign stars but added that they had to be given the chance to show off their new Euro-skills in the first team.

The England manager, Kevin Keegan, agreed. He said that only twenty out of the best fifty midfield players in the country were eligible to represent England. Other managers were also worried. Graham Taylor, who resurrected his career at Watford after he had been humiliated as England manager, attacked Arsène Wenger for recruiting so many foreign youngsters to the club's youth team. Taylor said that it was pointless to object to the importation of established foreign players – they were talented and good value – but he feared the long-term damage of Wenger's youth policy. Other managers pointed out that clubs like Arsenal, with increasing numbers of non-Europeans, would be punished because players from Africa, the Caribbean and South America would often be called up by their countries in the middle of the Premier League season to compete in competitions which no one in England had heard of. In January 2000, Arsenal, Chelsea and Liverpool, among others, lost some of their players for up to six weeks.

Brendan Batson, the deputy chief executive of the Professional Footballers' Association, cited the example of Chelsea's Jody Morris:

> Imagine how he feels when he sees Didier Deschamps, who was the captain of the World Cup winners, join the club. It's all very well saying that Jody has to be good enough to force himself into the team but how can he compete against a player who is the finished article? He doesn't have a chance. Young players need to forge their skills in competition but managers want results and import players rather than promote home talent. If you want a thriving domestic game you need to ensure that it has an identity. And that requires the development of young domestic players, not the buying of foreigners.

In the pre-Thatcher, pre-Sky, pre-Bosman era it was different. Compared with Continental clubs the English paid badly, the game was thuggish and the country was primitive. The English, meanwhile, considered foreigners odd. Northern Europeans, such as Dutchmen, were acceptable but southern Europeans were cheats and whingers and South Americans were strange creatures who did wonderful things in the sunshine but could not survive a cold night in Liverpool.

A few English players ventured abroad but usually returned quickly, moaning that their team-mates could not speak English, that they were expected to eat pasta and salad and that 'abroad' was generally lousy. This was a comment on footballers then – they were crass and insular – but by the late 1970s there were signs that some players realised that abroad was not a hostile environment. Kevin Keegan prospered in Hamburg; Chris Waddle and Glenn Hoddle were worshipped in Monaco; Graeme Souness and Ray

Wilkins enjoyed Italy. Gary Lineker spent a profitable three seasons at Barcelona in the late 1980s, although the manager played him in the wrong position. These players learnt the language and adapted to a different culture and did not pine for fish and chips and the lads back home; but others, notably Ian Rush, scuttled back after a season of misery not understanding what anyone was saying to them.

English clubs, meanwhile, were as slow as the players to accept that they could learn from the foreigners. In the late 1970s Bobby Robson of Ipswich recruited Arnold Muhren and Frans Thyssen from Holland; they transformed the team with their vision and passing. Spurs brought Ossie Ardiles, a tiny midfield genius and first-rate chess player, and Ricardo Villa, a heavy, bearded striker, from Argentina after they had helped win the World Cup in 1976. Villa soon returned home but Ardiles remained, adored by Spurs fans for his skill and courtesy.

By the 1980s, as the country opened its heart and mind to people whose native language was not English, more foreigners came here. Eric Cantona joined Leeds in 1992 from France, where he had squabbled constantly with managers and team-mates, before signing for Manchester United for £1.2 million in November 1992 (worth about £1.45 million in 2000; Cantona would have cost at least £15 million in 2000). He became one of United's most influential players and masterminded the club's run of four Premiership titles in five seasons. In the mid-1990s Jürgen Klinsmann had two spells with Spurs, the first for £24,000 a week, the second, in 1997–8, for a more generous £48,000 a week.

But even the best foreigners could be flawed. In 1996 Middlesbrough, recently promoted to the Premiership, with a multimillionaire chairman who was determined to turn the club into a giant, paid Juventus £7 million for Fabrizio Ravanelli, a striker whose prematurely white hair, which earned him the nickname 'White Feather', belied his age and his athleticism. He earned £42,000 a week but did not enjoy his time in the North East. He did not bother to learn English and, in between scoring a goal every other game, complained in the Italian newspapers that his team-mates were oafs. Middlesbrough were relegated and Ravanelli departed to Marseilles for £5.5 million. He had gone to Middlesbrough for the money but, once he realised that he hated it there, made it clear that he wanted to leave as soon as possible, whatever the cost. (Marseilles only paid him £25,000 a week.)

Other players were more mercenary. Nicolas Anelka forced Arsenal to sell him to Real Madrid, who had reportedly promised him £55,000 a week, for £23 million. Leeds also endured prolonged sulking from Jimmy Floyd Hasselbaink. They eventually sold him to Athletico Madrid, where he earned £45,000 a week. Leeds complained that Hasselbaink had been disloyal but this is hypocritical nonsense. The Premier League was set up because the old First Division clubs thought that the existing structures were not profitable enough. Foreigners did not come to England because they were interested in the museums or countryside; they were here to make money. And if clubs on the Continent offered more they would take it.

Leeds' chairman, Peter Risdale, did not see it like this. He raged that Hasselbaink was only interested in 'his wallet' and suggested that the British were not like this, which was ridiculous in view of the wage demands from local players which were leaked daily to the media.

It was, however, a general rule that the cheaper foreigners caused the most trouble. Harry Redknapp gave an hilarious account of his dealings with these cut-price players in his autobiography, *'Arry*. He said that West Ham had needed reinforcements for the 1996–7 season but prices had 'gone haywire' in England so he had been forced to look abroad. Apart from the fact that players were cheaper overseas the payment system was 'more flexible'; if West Ham bought a player in England they would have paid 50 per cent of the fee immediately and the balance in a year, but foreign clubs usually accepted a deposit and staggered payments.

Redknapp described his most spectacular flops. There was a Romanian who was frightened of being tackled and who once went shopping in London rather than play in a cup match at a lower division club in the North. There was the Dutchman who was psychologically unstable and who fled to Holland to live in a caravan; Redknapp eventually managed to 'unload' him to a small Dutch club. A Portuguese player was excellent but became extremely agitated when he was given a shirt with a squad number, 16, on the back, instead of his favourite number, 10. Another Portuguese was brilliant on the field but behaved like a pop star off it; Redknapp would probably have kept him but could not afford to do so.

Redknapp concluded that he had bought the football equivalent of 'second-hand cars with no MOT'. Morale in the dressing room had been affected by so many neurotics who had only come to West Ham for money. But he continued to shop abroad, only with more care.

Major clubs will continue to buy the best foreign players as long as they can afford to do so. The fans might grumble that they would prefer to be cheering players whose names they can pronounce but, on the other hand, they want a winning side more than anything else. Even if the income from television declines this will not affect the elite of the Premier League; by then they will be so wealthy that they will still claim the best players. And, if television in Britain decides that football has lost its appeal, there will probably be a similar reaction abroad and top English clubs will remain as proportionately rich as ever.

The smaller clubs will be the victims, unable to afford glamorous foreigners, starved of revenue from television and increasingly despised by a public brought up on a television and Internet diet of multinational Premiership magic.

At the beginning of the new millennium the Premiership clubs and the football authorities could see that there was a problem. There were indications that fans, who had been dazzled at first by so many foreigners, were becoming bored; where once it was a novelty to see Europeans and South Americans, now it was routine.

It was obvious that the foreigners did not care who they played for. This was true of English players – and always had been – but, somehow, it was more annoying when the mercenary was an Italian or a German. Clubs also fretted that the reliance on foreigners would affect the development of home talent.

The football authorities continued to mumble about limiting the number of foreigners clubs would be allowed to field, but this could not happen, and they knew it. Players from outside the European Union needed work permits but EU players could move wherever they liked; any attempt to stop them would be outlawed by the European courts.

Football in England will have to solve the problem without the help of the Government. There are various options, but they require determination, candour and self-sacrifice, qualities that are unknown in football. A club could ignore the temptation of the bargain-priced Frenchman and give the young local lad a chance. Clubs could agree not to play, say, more than four EU nationals. A club could accept that it will slip down the league while its young British players gain experience, rather than buy half a dozen veteran EU players. Football could do all this but it will not because it cares only about instant success, and damn the consequences.

Chapter Eight

Managers and Agents

Shortly after 5 o'clock every Saturday afternoon managers around the country meet the media to explain why they have won, drawn or lost their games of the day. A manager in the Premiership will be questioned by journalists from television, radio and national newspapers in an interview suite, after which the press can compare notes over complimentary drinks and snacks. In the lower divisions the media presence will probably consist of a solitary hack from the local rag in the cupboard which doubles as the manager's office and club laundry.

But no matter how humble the club or publication every reporter wants a row. This might be an attack on the manager's own players or the opposition but most outbursts are directed at the referee. The manager quivers, bites his lip, shrugs and frowns and says that he shouldn't say anything but his players worked their socks off and the fans deserved better. Then he will launch into the ref. He missed an obvious penalty. He should have sent off the number 10 'cos everyone could see he went over the ball. The ref ruined the game. He wasn't fit enough. People pay to see the players not the ref. We're professionals and these people are amateurs.

The higher the stakes the greater the fury. After being beaten by Manchester United, Roy Evans, then manager of Liverpool, normally a polite, quiet-spoken chap, was incandescent about a penalty which the referee, Steve Lodge, a local government officer from Barnsley, had awarded. 'The decision was diabolical,' Evans said. Another Premiership referee, Peter Jones, from Barrow, an account manager with BT, was told that he was 'entirely to blame' by Blackburn Rovers' manager, Roy Hodgson, after Rovers had been beaten by Chelsea. Jim Smith, the amusingly outspoken manager of Derby, was equally unimpressed by the refereeing of Graham Barber, a sales manager from Surrey, during a game against West Ham: 'The referee didn't lose control. He didn't have control in the first place.' Danny Wilson, manager of Sheffield Wednesday until he was sacked in March 2000, described referee Rob Harris from Oxford, as 'pathetic' after his team lost to Middlesbrough. George Graham of Spurs was often unhappy. He described Jeff Winter, a financial adviser, as 'very, very poor' after a game against Derby. He was also not impressed by Neale Barry, a manager with British Steel in Scunthorpe: after Neale had sent off a Blackburn player Graham complained that Spurs had struggled because 'it's harder to break down ten men'.

Gordon Strachan, Coventry City's manager, was convinced during the 1997–8 season that referees were punishing his team because the media had dismissed them as cloggers. Finally, after a match against Arsenal, he challenged the FA to discipline him: 'The referee today was an absolute joke. The standard of entertainment and football is getting higher all the time but the standard of refereeing is way down. If the FA wants to come after me it can.' The FA did not take up his invitation and, after Coventry's results improved, Strachan calmed down.

After firing insults at the referee, the Premiership manager on a four-year contract worth £1.2 million a year, plus bonuses, can swop jokes over drinks with his counterpart, an old mate from the England team, and be congratulated or consoled by the directors in the boardroom. He might nip down to the dressing room to talk to the players, though he will probably leave this chore to his assistant manager and coaches. In his office he might call a few well-connected agents abroad because the game that afternoon has emphasised that he has to get a right-sided midfielder who can hold the ball up. He might call Mario in Rome, Gunnar in Oslo, Jesper in Stockholm, or maybe Erik, the guy in Johannesburg who says that he's plugged into the black clubs, which have loads of great talent, to see if they have any ideas. Providing there is no transfer fee money will not be a problem. The basic wage will be £15,000 a week for a kid and up to £30,000 for an international. And the agent will get a tasty commission for setting up the deal. Finally, he will climb into his club Mercedes, BMW or Jaguar for the drive to his £2 million home. Next day he might be flying to London to be the studio analyst for the Arsenal–Chelsea game. It will only pay a couple of grand but will be good PR and he can take the opportunity to have dinner with his accountant who wants to discuss a new tax avoidance scheme.

A manager in the Second or Third Division, on an annual salary of £30,000 plus a bonus of £5,000 for promotion, might share a beer with the rival manager who can't stay long because the team have a long drive back south and the weather's filthy. Then he will help his coach collect the kit and load the washing machine in his office. As he is leaving, the chairman will tell him that the bank has approved an extension on the overdraft, so the wages will be paid next month. He will return to the office, now vibrating from the washing machine, and call the agent in London who has promised him the Premiership goalie with a gambling problem on a free transfer, providing that he is bunged a grand. No way, says the manager: we might be crap but we're not bent. Then he walks to his car, a 1991 Ford Escort, and prays that it will start.

Managers reflect the range of humanity: the decent, the brutal, the selfish and the selfless, the honest and dishonest. Some live like pop stars; many are quiet, family men. A few are multimillionaires; most fret every time interest rates go up. If they are sacked they know that there is a 50 per cent chance that they will not work again. One hundred and thirty-five managers were fired by the seventy-two Nationwide League clubs in three seasons in the late 1990s and of that number only half found another job in the game. There are dozens of applications for every managerial opening, even at a bankrupt minnow.

Competition is always intense: apart from cranks and supporters, there are ex-Premiership players who haven't banked enough in their careers to retire, assistant managers and coaches from big clubs who want to run their own show, and veteran managers who once won the FA Cup or First Division title and who have been filling in time as television pundits. Small clubs should always go for the man who can coach players of limited ability, barter on the transfer market and persuade local businesses to donate match balls; but often they choose a household name because publicity is everything today.

In the past football managers had to manipulate directors – most of whom knew little about football, apart from the fact that it was prestigious to be on the board of the local club – and discipline players, working-class young men who often drank heavily, gambled and womanised. Managers ran everything – training, team selection and transfers – and were known as Boss. But they were not wealthy men. They were ordinary employees. Everyone knew their place: directors swanked, managers ordered and players did as they were told and were sold if they did not.

This was the football of managerial legends like Bill Nicholson, Bill Shankly, Jock Stein, Brian Clough and Bob Paisley. It was the world of black and white television, when crowds of 50,000 swayed on the terraces while players slogged it out on mud heaps, tackling with a ferocity that would earn them a red card today. These managers believed that a player was only as good as his last game. If one was injured he was not earning his wages and had to be pushed back to fitness as soon as possible, even if that meant pumping him with painkillers. But, faced with today's designer-suited young Premiership managers on annual salaries of £1 million, it is tempting to romanticise these gruff old warriors as symbols of a purer past.

Bill Shankly was a particular favourite and his quotes pepper books on football. Once he told Ian St John, his Scottish forward, 'Don't overeat and don't lose your accent.' He said of Tommy

Smith that he could 'start a riot in a graveyard'. When Smith was injured Shankly told him; 'What do you mean you've hurt your knee? It's Liverpool's knee.' The press adored Shankly because he always delivered glorious one-liners. On the eve of a derby match with Everton he said, 'If Everton were playing at the bottom of my garden then I'd close the curtains.'

There was Brian Clough, who managed Nottingham Forest from 1975 until 1993. For many years he was a colossus but he ended as a pathetic remnant of the old football. He had turned a struggling Second Division team into the champions of England and Europe but his management style was based on total independence – which became unacceptable as soon as clubs became businesses – and subservient players – not the independently wealthy young men of the late 1980s and 1990s. Clough could not cope and he retired, discredited and bloated from what he admitted had been 'one glass of wine too many from time to time'.

Sir Alf Ramsey, the only England manager to win the World Cup, was often downright rude to the media and would have been regarded as a public relations disaster by today's image-obsessed Premiership clubs. But he turned Ipswich Town, a small, struggling Third Division South club, into First Division champions in the 1961–2 season and convinced a good but not a great England team that it could beat the world.

He was born in 1920 in Dagenham, east London, the son of a hay and straw merchant. The war meant that he did not become a professional player until he was twenty-six, when he signed for Southampton on £6 a week in the summer (worth about £130 in 2000) and £8 during the season (£176 in 2000). He won the first of thirty-two England caps and then moved to Spurs, where he became one of the most cultured full backs in the country. In 1955 he became manager of Ipswich.

Ipswich's chairman at the time was John Cobbold, described by Jimmy Greaves, arguably England's most naturally gifted striker, as 'a wonderfully eccentric, warm and likeable Old Etonian who might have stepped out of the pages of a P.G. Wodehouse book'. A reporter once asked Cobbold how he was coping with a crisis – Ipswich were doing badly at the time – and he replied, 'A crisis at Ipswich, dear boy, is when the white wine served in the boardroom is not sufficiently chilled.'

There was little money available so Ramsey had to improve the existing players – which he did – or pick up underpriced ones from other clubs: his most expensive signing cost £12,500, which was cheap even in the 1950s. Above all, he was a coach and a tactician but Ipswich taught him, too, that for a small club to be successful everyone, from the star striker to the tea lady, had to feel that they were appreciated.

Ramsey became England manager in 1963 and, over the next eleven years, demonstrated a Shanklyesque gift for memorable quotes. When he landed at Glasgow airport for the annual fixture against Scotland a local journalist bade him 'Welcome to Scotland, Mr Ramsey.' He replied, 'You must be bloody joking.' A South American journalist once greeted him with an outstretched hand and a smile, 'Mr Ramsey, you remember me . . .' Ramsey snapped, 'Yes, you're a pest.' The day after England won the World Cup he was asked for his thoughts by three journalists: 'Gentlemen, this is my day off,' he said.

Ramsey treated his England players like adults who had a responsibility to the public. If they let him down once they were warned; twice and they were out. There were no exceptions, not even his captain, Bobby Moore, the finest defender in the history of the English game. Ramsey was treated with contempt by the FA, elderly snobs who thought that all managers, especially chaps who came from the East End, were clods. His bonus for winning the World Cup was £5,000 and, when he was sacked in May 1974 he was on an annual salary of £7,200, a third of the average salary of a top manager. His 'compensation' package was a lump sum of £8,000 and an annual pension of £1,200, roughly the price of one of Kevin Keegan's suits on the eve of Euro 2000.

Don Revie, the former Leeds manager who was in charge of England from 1974 to 1977, was destroyed by resentment that he had earned so little from football. Like Ramsey he had learnt management at a struggling club; the Leeds United he joined as player-manager in December 1958 was in the Second Division and was heading for the Third. Revie built an extraordinary team, one that was as complex as him, and capable of breathtaking skill but also shocking cynicism. He was religious – he used to urge his England players to pray before they went to bed – but so materialistic that he eventually fled to Dubai in 1977 to make the fortune which he thought that he deserved. Today Revie could have stayed at home because he would have been a millionaire.

Bobby Robson, England manager from 1982 to 1990, straddled the two footballs, from the unfashionable, working-class sport watched by morons and played by louts, to today's glamorous, multimillion pound leisure industry. In August 1999, long past retirement age, Robson was summoned by Newcastle to rescue them after a disastrous year under Ruud Gullit; to the surprise of the new football he showed that qualities such as honesty, loyalty and humility, derided as old-fashioned, still had a place.

Robson had been a naturally gifted half back but he was also a superb coach, able to convert journeymen into top-class players. Like Ramsey and Revie, he had had a tough apprenticeship in management. After being sacked by Fulham he took charge of Ipswich and, in thirteen years, made the club synonymous with stylish, attacking football. His reign as England manager, which ended in Turin in July 1990 with the World Cup semi-final against West Germany, saw players become superstars. But Robson survived, suggesting that legends such as Ramsey might have been able to adapt to a dressing room full of young men who lived in mansions and drove Porsches.

In general, however, most naturally brilliant players make bad managers because football has been so easy for them. A great manager is a man who can turn an ordinary player into a good one, and a good player into a world-class performer. Partly this involves coaching but it is also about 'motivation'; in the days before

151

£1,000-a-day 'self-awareness' courses run by ex-England rugby captains it was called hard graft.

There are always exceptions, though, to any generalisation. Glenn Hoddle, the former Spurs and England midfielder who possessed sublime talent, became a first-rate coach, at Swindon and then at Chelsea. But Hoddle was destroyed as England manager by vanity (he insisted on showing his squad during training sessions that he was still a great player) and by stupidity (he regularly shared his 'thoughts' on spiritualism with the media). Kevin Keegan, his successor as England coach, was shrewder. Keegan's problem was that, unlike Ramsey and Robson, he had only managed clubs – Newcastle and Fulham – where money had never been a problem, and had never been forced to hide the deficiencies of ordinary players with sophisticated tactics.

A few Premiership managers in 2000 come over as successors to Shankly and the rest. Manchester United's Sir Alex Ferguson, perhaps the greatest manager in the history of English football, learnt management at impoverished East Stirling and St Mirren before he moved to Aberdeen, and then to Manchester.

In the 1980s Harry Redknapp managed Bournemouth, a team constantly on the verge of bankruptcy, before he returned to West Ham, where he had been a not-very-effective winger in the 1960s. The skills which Redknapp acquired at Bournemouth – making do with not very much and convincing players that they were better than they were – transformed West Ham from a club which seemed destined to slip out of the Premiership into one that was a member of its second tier, behind the elite of Manchester United, Arsenal, Leeds and Chelsea. But Redknapp also has perspective. He knows what it is like to be broke and appreciates the rewards of the new football. But he is too canny to lecture young players on their good fortune, knowing that they would dismiss him as a silly old sod. If they take the money and the perks for granted, he jettisons them quietly, usually at a profit. Ferguson is the same. Although United's players earn huge salaries, Ferguson weeds out the shirkers; his players have to work for their wages, as if their lives depend on winning.

Redknapp concedes that most players in the 1960s lived on fish and chips and beer, hardly the perfect diet for athletes, and believes that today's players, who eat pasta and drink mineral water, are stronger, fitter and more agile mentally. He does not begrudge players their enormous salaries. Good luck to them, he says, because their careers are so short. He does not want to see them end up like Bobby Moore, his former captain at West Ham: 'He was sitting in the back of the stands at Grimsby, eating fish and chips out of a newspaper and freezing his nuts off, just to earn a couple of bob helping out a radio station. This was the England captain who lifted the World Cup but no one gave a shit.' Like Ferguson, Redknapp frequently grumbles about his finances: 'It's criminal that we could be earning less than a player not even guaranteed a place in the first team. I'm glad to say that recently our lot has improved but it still has further to go before I'm completely happy. Given the responsibility I must shoulder, the constant pressure I'm under, surely my pay should be on a par with my top players.'

Alan Smith was manager of Crystal Palace from 1993 to 1995 and led the club to the Premier League. But they were relegated immediately and, by February 2000, were in administration. Smith was appalled by the behaviour of many modern players:

Most players come from working-class backgrounds and I am sure they have trouble relating the job they do to the amount of money they earn. Often I argued with players about petty amounts of money that would have astonished supporters. It's like coming across a millionaire who doesn't tip lowly paid waiters or porters. I sometimes wonder why agents, who give so much financial advice to their clients, don't spend a little more time advising them how their public image can be affected by what appears to be money grabbing.

Once I took on loan an international player who was one of the top earners in the game, on £6,000 per week. As well as his salary we paid his travel and hotel bills, but were surprised to find that he had included contraceptives on his room expenses. When we queried this item, he argued that it was a valid expense because he was away from home, and it was only after I suggested we discuss the matter with his wife in the North of England that he agreed to take responsibility for the cost of his condoms.

Some players consider playing kit as another 'perk' of the job. Kit managers up and down the country have always had problems with shirts and tracksuits going missing and one of my former players amazed me. I discovered after a game at Liverpool that twenty-four new tracksuits had gone, and was not unduly surprised to hear of them turning up in a sports shop in a London market. I understand that the same player also 'borrowed' a full kit from another leading club after we had sold him. I'll always remember him as the man who returned my wife's car after we'd lent it to him for a week – but with the radio missing. He was earning around £150,000 at the time.

One manager, meanwhile, decided that it was time to share in football's financial boom. Rather than being a mere employee he wanted real money, which meant owning a slice of a club. He was Terry Venables, who had been the midfield brain of Tommy Docherty's flamboyant Chelsea of the 1960s and who had played twice for England.

Venables was one of the most interesting characters in football in the 1990s. He was an outstanding coach, a sparkling television pundit and was popular with football writers, who found him funny and frank. But Venables also believed that he was a businessman, which he was not. He wanted power as well as glory, and power was money. He made his reputation as a coach in the late 1970s when he managed Crystal Palace, a club which had always promised to become a Spurs, Arsenal or Chelsea but had never quite done so. Palace won promotion to the First Division in 1979, before a crowd of 51,000 at Selhurst Park, and were dubbed 'the team of the Eighties'. But they struggled and he decamped to Queen's Park Rangers, where he remained for four years.

Queen's Park Rangers' chairman was Jim Gregory, an East Ender who made a fortune in the motor trade. It was a temptestuous relationship but it worked. Gregory ran the club and Venables coached the players, which was what he was good at. Rangers were promoted to the First Division, reached an FA Cup Final and seemed destined to become a major force in English football. In 1984, however, Venables decided that he needed a bigger stage – and more money – and took command at Barcelona.

Barcelona was a revelation. It was the symbol of Catalonia's independence from the central government in Madrid and drew support from a region, not simply the city. It had a stadium, the Nou Camp, which was regularly packed with 110,000 people, many of whom were middle-class families. It had a guaranteed annual income of millions of pounds from members, who were the equivalent of ultra-loyal English season ticket holders. Unlike most clubs in England, where the manager was involved in transfers and contracts, Barcelona's coach was responsible only for the players. Venables thought that a major English club could be developed like this, with him as the supreme boss.

In Venables' first season, Barcelona won the Spanish league for the first time in eleven years. This was a promising start but Barcelona's fans expected more. In 1986 the club reached the European Cup Final, but lost to a Romanian team which was supposed to roll over and surrender. That was the end of Venables and in 1987 he returned to London to become manager at Spurs. For the next four years he seemed content as he built the kind of elegant team that Spurs fans demanded. He transformed Paul Gascoigne into the finest creative midfield player in the country and resurrected the career of Gary Lineker.

In autumn 1990 it emerged that Spurs had debts of £18 million, thanks to building a new East Stand and the failure of its 'merchandising and leisurewear arms'. This was the opportunity that Venables had been waiting for: he would take control and turn

Spurs into the Barcelona of north London. And he would become rich. Backed by Alan Sugar, Venables became the club's chief executive. But Sugar had no intention of letting Venables run anything other than the football team; his money had bought Spurs and it was his club. Inevitably the two fell out and soon writs were being hurled between their lawyers. It would be dangerous – both men are litigious – to say more here but it is safe to report that Venables lost and was forced to leave the club in 1993. Football writers were sympathetic. Sugar was a ruthless businessman who had trampled over Terry, El Tel, the maestro of Spain. But reporters who knew nothing about football doubted this and began digging. Their investigations revealed that Venables' business methods were, at best, unorthodox. Venables protested his innocence and said that there was a media conspiracy against him, which was improbable since the attack on him was led by the BBC's flagship current affairs programme, *Panorama*, which has the most rigorous ethical guidelines in journalism.

Venables the Football Coach, however, was needed by England, who had just failed to qualify for the 1994 World Cup finals in the USA. Graham Taylor, a decent man who had been hopelessly out of his depth as an international manager, had resigned, and the FA, under pressure from Venables' friends in the media, offered him a one-year contract. Many in the FA wanted nothing to do with someone whose business affairs had attracted the attention of crack investigative reporters, but he was the only man who could produce a team that would not be an embarrassment in the European Championship in England in 1996. After further discussions the FA offered him a two-year contract but it hardly represented a vote of confidence in Venables because England managers were normally given four-year deals, taking in a World Cup and a European Championship. To Venables' irritation the FA also inserted a clause saying that they could dismiss him if his 'legal difficulties' embarrassed the association. The final insult was that he would be given the title of coach, not manager.

By December 1995 Venables felt that he had done enough to

merit a new, and improved, contract which would take him through to the World Cup in France in 1998. But the FA refused. They said that it would be better to see how the team fared in Euro '96 the following summer, though it was rumoured at the time that they were stalling because they knew that the Department of Trade and Industry would be publishing a report on Venables' business affairs in January. Venables was incensed and announced that he would be 'resigning' after Euro '96, though the truth was less dramatic; his contract would simply have ended then. The FA squirmed as Venables' allies in the media attacked them for hounding a man because of unproved allegations which had nothing to do with his abilities as a coach. But the DTI report on Venables was more savage than even his fiercest critics imagined it would be: he was banned for seven years from being a company director. Ordinary fans, however, did not care about this; everyone had problems with tax and VAT and all that mattered was having a world-class England team.

Venables should have packed away his pocket calculator and concentrated on football, but he was determined to prove everyone wrong. After Euro '96 he tried again to become a mogul. In August that year John Gregory, the son of Venables' old pal from QPR, was chairman of Portsmouth, an ailing First Division club. He invited Venables to help him raise investment to restore the club. The details of this unhappy relationship are as complex and legally fraught as anything that happened at Spurs.

Having failed to become the multimillionaire saviour of Portsmouth, Venables decided to return to Crystal Palace, where he had begun his managerial career. The story of his seven months at Selhurst Park shows how the brains of intelligent men can turn to mush when they step inside football clubs, as if they have been infected by a virus which destroys common sense. Unlike at Spurs and Portsmouth, it is easy to explain what happened, though it is difficult to understand why a successful businessman, Mark Goldberg, decided to pay £22.8 million for a club which had just been relegated from the Premiership. Other clubs with less potential than Palace had also been snapped up by businessmen but they had always acquired tangible assets, such as a stadium. Goldberg, however, a lifelong Palace fan, had bought the name, the players, mounting debts and an uncertain future. Ron Noades, the outgoing chairman, walked away from Palace with £20 million but retained ownership of Selhurst Park and the training ground.

Goldberg behaved as if money grew in his back garden. He spent millions of pounds on Palace. He said that he had 'a five-year plan' to turn it into a European super-club, which even fanatical Palace fans knew was nonsense. He employed an IT manager, a human resources manager, an Internet specialist and a public relations team. He also employed a doctor, assorted fitness experts, a masseur, five physiotherapists, a nutritionist and a cook. A staff like this would be considered excessive in the Premiership but at a club like Palace it was surreal.

His fantasy that Palace was a major force in world football was best illustrated, however, by his relationship with Venables. Since Palace was a great club it had to have the ex-England coach, no matter how much this cost. The contract which he agreed with Venables was astonishing even by the standards of football.

Venables had been paid £135,000 for discussing the possibility of joining Palace. His annual salary was £750,000, after tax, paid annually and in advance. He would receive an unsecured, interest-free loan of £500,000 and a house, worth £650,000, in which he would 'retain the equity interest'. He would have a company Mercedes. He would be paid £20,000 'relocation expenses'. He would be paid a '6 per cent royalty on the use of his image' and would be allowed to remain a consultant to the Australian Football Association. Goldberg would make available £10 million for transfers during the 1998–9 season and £5 million during the next two seasons. But Venables would get 'a 5 per cent bonus on amounts not spent on transfers'. Palace would have an annual salary budget of £10 million.

It was absolutely mad. But Venables assumed that in Goldberg he had simply found someone who appreciated his value and in June 1998 he joined Palace. Seven months later he departed, complaining that, sadly, Goldberg did not have the funds to match his ambitions. In early March, Goldberg summoned the administrators, who discovered that Palace had debts of £20 million, which Goldberg could not pay. The cost cutting which followed was savage: forty-six backroom staff went; some players were sold at bargain prices and others, whom no one wanted, were 'released'. By the summer of 1999 the creditors were lining up, including Venables, who wanted his five-year contract, worth £6.9 million, to be honoured.

Venables could not be blamed for any of this. He was only doing what came naturally to him: getting his share of the money from a sport which had become a multimillion pound industry. But the manager who represented the worst of the new football of designer suits, private jets and chauffeured limousines was Ruud Gullit. He swept into Newcastle in August 1998, promising 'sexy' football, and trophies; a year later he resigned. Instead of apologising to the most loyal supporters in the country for his failure to bring anything apart from overpriced and overpaid foreign players to St James' Park he was self-pitying and condescending.

The Gullit saga is more than the story of a prodigiously talented player who was an awful manager; it is also about an industry, and a country, which was overawed by European chic. Gullit was born in Amsterdam in 1962, the son of a Dutch West Indian father and a Dutch mother. At the age of sixteen he was playing for Haarlem, a small professional club. In 1981, aged nineteen, he made his debut for Holland. He dominated European football for the next fourteen years. He was tall, strong and fast but he also had remarkable balance and agility. He was also handsome, articulate (he picked up languages as casually as his team-mates collected cars) and intelligent. Unfortunately, he was aware of all this. As he moved from one European giant to another – Feyenoord, PSV Eindhoven, Milan – filling his trophy cabinet with medals, he became increasingly difficult. He was always right and, if his team was failing, it was because the manager, the coaches, the other players were useless. By his early thirties he was also rich, which further inflated his ego.

In 1995 Glenn Hoddle signed him for Chelsea. Gullit was past his best as a player but still made many Premiership players look like donkeys. But his popularity with fans and the media had little to do with his performances on the pitch. Here was a multimillionaire who spoke six languages, looked like James Bond with dreadlocks and oozed class. To a sport, and a country, which had always been in awe of European elegance Gullit's presence at Stamford Bridge was a compliment and a lesson; yes, the country sighed, *this* is what we want to be like.

In May 1996 Hoddle left to take over England and Gullit became Chelsea's player-coach. At first everything went well. He introduced Continental training techniques and bought players from abroad. They came for the money but they also brought European habits and attitudes; British players watched agog as the foreigners chomped pasta, sipped mineral water, practised endlessly on the training ground, read books, studied English and talked to journalists without asking for money. In May 1997 Chelsea won the FA Cup when they beat Middlesbrough 2-0.

But Gullit had served his purpose. By New Year 1998 the game had absorbed dozens more foreigners, including Arsène Wenger, the studious Frenchman who had taken charge at Arsenal in November 1996. Compared with Wenger, Gullit seemed cocky and aloof. Chelsea players complained that he rarely spoke to them and was so busy with his business interests that he was an occasional visitor to the training ground. But Gullit did not care. He shrugged when journalists asked him why he did not spend more time at the club; he saw himself as a figurehead, who could not be expected to waste his time with the minutiae of management. He was sacked in February 1998 after demanding a massive pay rise.

That should have been the end of his career in English football. He tried to persuade another London club to employ him, but by now everyone knew that he saw management as one of many elements in his business portfolio, along with modelling, making television advertisements and developing his own clothing range. He also spent much of his time in Amsterdam with his girlfriend, Estelle, the niece of Johan Cruyff. In summer 1998 the BBC employed him as a pundit during the World Cup. He was not a success with his fellow-pundits or with the viewers; his self-confidence seemed no more than arrogance.

A year later Newcastle summoned him after Kenny Dalglish was fired. Even by the standards of football clubs this was a stupid appointment. Newcastle should have employed an experienced manager, who understood that United was more than a mere football club to the city; to Geordies it was proof that, while many of them might be unemployed, they were as good as anyone else. Instead they hired Gullit for £1 million a year and hoped that he would make the club and the city fashionable.

Gullit thought that they were lucky to have him. He had no intention of moving permanently to a provincial city and was always popping down to London or to Amsterdam, where his girlfriend lived. Meanwhile, he spent £32.5 million on players, mostly foreigners who were only interested in their pay cheques. To be fair, he recouped £22.5 million but the players whom he sold included some of the team's best performers, such as David Batty. His biggest mistake, however, was to offend United's hero, Alan Shearer. Shearer had joined the club in 1996 in preference to Manchester United, because he was a Geordie and, though he could be surly, no one doubted that he loved Newcastle. But Gullit thought that he was more powerful than Shearer, which was a fatal error.

By August 1999 Gullit's team had only won eleven Premiership matches out of forty-one, and had not won since April the previous season. In August Sunderland won 2-1 at St James' Park, with Shearer, talisman and club captain, dropped to substitute. That match doomed Gullit. In his resignation statement he moaned about 'press intrusion', which was ridiculous from a man who had courted publicity so assiduously, and thanked 'all the restaurants where I have been for their marvellous food and hospitality', as if they should be flattered by the approval of a gourmet like him.

No one mourned Gullit's departure. One local journalist wrote that fans were asking, 'Just what have we done to deserve a team of pampered £20,000-a-week foreigners who play with so little passion and pride?' He concluded, 'If there was ever a marriage made in hell it was the one between the Newcastle manager, Gullit, in his designer suits, pseudo-soccer babble and jet-set lifestyle and Shearer, the son of a sheet metal worker. Gullit was the wrong man in the wrong job at the wrong time.'

But clubs continued to employ well-known ex-players as managers. Some were a success, like Peter Reid, formerly a tenacious midfielder with Everton, at Sunderland, but others, notably John Barnes, the ex-Liverpool winger, who was sacked in February 2000 as coach of Celtic, were a disaster.

John Barnwell, chief executive of the League Managers' Association, told me that the game in England was still a shambles; in Europe managers and coaches – and there was a clear distinction between the two – had to be qualified but English clubs did not care about this. Some clubs had moved towards the European model but in others the manager was the Boss, even if he thought that a plc was the latest high performance Ferrari.

Barnwell had learnt the traditional way. After playing for Arsenal, Nottingham Forest and Sheffield United he began at the bottom of the managerial ladder with Peterborough. Then he moved up to Wolves. He said that in a small club a manager had to do everything – train players, arrange transfers and organise marketing and publicity – and could never blame anyone else if errors were made.

But he said that major clubs today demanded big-name coaches, which meant that they employed ex-players who did not have basic coaching qualifications and had no idea how a modern business works. Barnwell believed it was time for English football to accept the continental model: managers should have degrees in business administration and coaches should be required to have FA certificates and a basic understanding of business. The LMA was trying to organise courses with universities in London and Lancashire but football was notoriously conservative and, he added sadly, it would take a long time to change its culture of ignorance.

Like so much today that seems to have been with us for ever – video recorders, mobile phones, computers and cash points – the sports agent is a recent invention. The first was the American Mark McCormack, founder of the International Management Group (IMG). McCormack launched his business in the late 1950s, when he realised that the golfer Arnold Palmer was an advertisement waiting to happen. The prize money in golf was respectable but McCormack saw that this should only be a small proportion of a champion's earnings; golfers – and tennis players – in the States were well off and spent a fortune on equipment. McCormack understood that weekend players whose tee shots always ended up in the rough or who hit serves that flopped over the net at 10 mph believed that they would become champions if their clubs and rackets bore the name of a star. But that was only the start.

In 1967 McCormack summed up his philosophy:

It is now possible not only to play your golf with Arnold Palmer clubs, while dressed from cleat to umbrella tip in Palmer clothes . . . but to have the Palmer image at your elbow in countless other ways. You can buy your insurance from a Palmer agency, stay in a Palmer-owned motel, buy a Palmer lot to build your home on, push a Palmer-approved lawn mower, read a Palmer book, newspaper column or pamphlet, be catered for by a Palmer maid, listen to Palmer music and send your suit to a Palmer dry cleaner. You can shave with his lather, spray on his deodorant, drink his favourite soft drink, fly his preferred airline, buy his approved corporate jet, eat his candy bar, order your stock certificates through him and cut up wood with his power tools.

IMG concentrated on individual sports, such as golf, tennis and motor racing, but soon moved into American team games. Companies had such huge advertising budgets that new heroes were created, though none had the monumental stature of Palmer, who became one of the most famous and respected men in the country.

Then IMG expanded worldwide and became as powerful as the governing bodies of the sports whose stars were represented by it. In the 1980s, for example, the broadsheet press in Britain asked whether McCormack, rather than the All England Lawn Club, ran Wimbledon. But football in England was of no interest to him.

The World Cup in Italy in 1990, the creation of the Premier League in the early 1990s and the subsequent deal with satellite television changed everything. IMG and its rivals moved into football. An agency negotiated contracts with clubs and sponsors, set up book deals, newspaper columns and coaching videos, organised tax avoidance and pensions and handled public relations, to ensure that a player had a saleable image, whether it was as a rebel, such as Eric Cantona, whom Nike liked because it gave the company 'street cred' with teenagers, or a Mr Clean, such as Gary Lineker, employed by Walkers crisps to enhance their image as manufacturers of wholesome food. Good agents ensured that a player did not have to work again after he retired; a bad one, and there were many, wanted to make as much money as possible, and didn't care what happened to the player when it was all over.

Managers, particularly in the Premiership, frequently complain that agents are destroying the game by agitating for players under contract to leave a club (because every move generates commission) and by demanding massive salaries for their clients. But football is a bazaar, open three hundred and sixty-five days a year. One in five English league professionals move clubs every season, as managers dump disruptive, unfit or out-of-form players and find new ones. And agents are the vital middlemen, as Harry Redknapp explained in his autobiography:

I know most fans think agents are frowned upon by those of us inside football, but nowadays they are an integral part of a transfer. Most managers are happy to negotiate with agents because they recognise them as a necessary evil. For instance the moment I ring a manager and tell him that I'm releasing one of my players, the value automatically goes down. But if an agent puts the word around, something like 'I hear West Ham may be prepared to sell so and so. I don't think West Ham want to lose him but I hear he's desperate to get away', then the asking price will remain at the level you want.

In 2000 it was estimated that there were hundreds of agents, ranging from respected companies, like IMG, to one-man outfits with a post office box for a business address, around the world. In England alone eighty agents were licensed by FIFA, for a bond of about £80,000, to broker transfers within the country and abroad, while another forty-two agents could only handle transfers within the country, in return for a bond of £30,000. But one leading agent told me that there were dozens more who did not exist officially.

Top agents nurture players through their careers. Phil Smith, of First Artist Corporation, based in Middlesex, whose clients included Les Ferdinand of Spurs, Mark Bosnich of Manchester United and Gianfranco Zola of Chelsea, said that good agents were not interested in short-term gains: 'Sometimes you don't want too good a contract because that might harm a player's development. But sometimes you go for the jugular. The idea is to make sure that the player earns so much that he never has to work again when he retires.' Smith said that the rewards for the leading players are 'staggering' – and will become even larger: 'It's only right that the players benefit because they are the ones putting bums on seats. These players know that they have to get it right. The old days are over. They have to treat their bodies like temples. We tell 'em to enjoy their money but we advise them to lock most of it away. And most are sensible and listen to us.'

Smith said that it was absurd for clubs and managers to complain that agents were squeezing too much money out of the game; it was a free market and players were paid what they deserve. But he added that football was fracturing, into an elite and the rest. Logic dictated that there would be two Premier Leagues, of sixteen clubs each, and that the rest would become nurseries for the elite and would play in regional leagues.

Another FIFA-licensed agent, Hayden Evans, of HN Sports and Entertainment Ltd of Leeds, who had irritated Premiership managers by demanding so much for his clients, thought that the system was splendid: 'The ceiling is determined by television's money, not the agents. Television exposure brings the clubs all their sponsorship. Everything stems from television. My argument is with those clubs and managers who criticise us yet who, that day, will probably be sitting down with an agent they hate and a player they think is greedy. But they've decided they must have him and they are prepared to sell their soul to the Devil to get him. It's hypocrisy.'

Like many agents, Evans was often contacted by clubs around the world, searching for players who could perform a certain role. If he found the right player the club would pay him a fee. No one, he said, wanted to return to the days when clubs and players negotiated directly with each other. He also insisted that players realised that he would be loyal throughout their careers, while clubs would dump them as soon as it was convenient: 'A club will sell a player if it suits them but we will always be there.'

David Speedie, once a lively and aggressive player with Chelsea, became a FIFA-recognised agent after he retired in the mid-1990s. He said that his job was to ensure that his clients could live in comfort for the rest of their lives: 'I make sure that players realise that it will end one day and to plan for that.' Other agents said that they were 'tough' with players: 'They used to get it and spend it. We tell them that they had better take our advice. We ask them what they need for pocket money – they're young guys and want to enjoy themselves – but we invest the rest,' said one.

Companies like First Artist Corporation, with lawyers, account-ants and marketing specialists, belong to the new football. But before the boom there was another game, of undeclared bonuses, loans and dodgy deals involving houses owned by clubs. By the early 1990s, however, as money poured into the game, the Inland Revenue began to take an interest. Swindon Town forfeited promotion to the First Division after it emerged that the club had made tax-free payments to players. Spurs were also found guilty of 'financial irregularities'. But most fans thought that it wasn't such a bad thing to fiddle the taxman. They were shocked, though, to discover that corruption and greed, involving unimaginable sums, were endemic in the sport. This time the guilty men were not club chairmen and secretaries whom no one cared about, but a manager who was a hero to millions: Arsenal's George Graham, who had won the First Division title twice, the FA Cup and the European Cup Winners' Cup since joining the club in 1986.

The story dribbled out in 1994. In December 1991 Graham had received £140,000 in cash from a Norwegian agent, Rune Hauge, 'for helping open doors in England'. In August 1992, Hauge sent Graham a bank draft for £285,000. Graham deposited both sums in an offshore trust fund for his children, which at least showed that he cared about his family. The football authorities – and Arsenal, a club which had always taken pride in its probity – were not pleased and launched an investigation. It was established that the two payments were 'bungs' linked to Arsenal's purchase of two Scandinavian players. Graham had taken the money as his cut, which led to Arsenal sacking him in February 1995 without compensation. He protested his innocence – he insisted that he had thought the money was a gift – and repaid the full amount, with interest, to Arsenal. He was banned from the game for a year. Hauge was also struck off FIFA's list of approved agents.

It was hard to believe that this was an isolated incident; Graham had always been considered a decent man, unlike some of his colleagues, who were rumoured to have become millionaires through illicit deals. But football closed ranks after the scandal; three years later the FA said that its investigation into bungs had revealed that the sport was clean, apart from one of Graham's assistants who had also been rewarded by Hauge. The media howled that this was a cover-up but, without the irrefutable evidence required under British libel law, could not say more.

FA officials privately accepted that corruption had been a problem in the early 1990s, though proving it was another matter. They insisted that the Graham affair had had the desired effect: managers, agents and players now realised that they could be caught and ruined. There were other factors. The major clubs had become businesses by the mid-1990s, run by accountants. In the era of the £100,000 transfer and £1,000-a-week salaries it had been easy to skim money but it required the ingenuity of a professional fraudster rather than simple greed to do this when the figures involved were so vast.

But money attracts crooks and no one believed that the sport had suddenly become 100 per cent honest. The growth of transfers to England from countries where business was conducted in what might be called an 'informal manner' brought new problems. For example, in his autobiography Sir Alex Ferguson said that he had not enjoyed dealing with a Russian agent, who was under the mistaken impression that Ferguson was as corrupt as he was. Ferguson said that he was appalled when the man gave him an envelope containing £40,000 in 1995, for reasons which were not clear; Ferguson told the club solicitor and lodged the money in the club safe, until he returned it to the agent. Gordon Taylor, chief executive of the PFA, thought that incidents like this were a warning that clubs in England had to be wary when they dealt with foreign agents. He was especially worried about developing nations where there was a tradition of 'personal commissions'. He said: 'Many managers have told me of their concern over signing foreign players. For lurking within the waters of the foreign player market are the foreign agents and questionable deals. There are so many opportunities for foreign clubs dealing in big sums to give so-called authority to middlemen to negotiate on their behalf. And you find the money is being paid into a Swiss bank rather than going directly to the club. Inevitably, you wonder where that money is ending up.'

David O'Leary of Leeds was so disgusted by the activities of agents that, in summer 1999, he invited a journalist from the *Daily Express* to inspect the evidence; there, on his desk, was a pile of faxes from agents offering him players who were still under contract to other clubs. He did not know whether these agents even represented the players; unscrupulous operators often tried to set up a deal and, after a club had bitten, approached the player and demanded a cut of the transfer which he had just set up.

Bryan Robson, the manager of Middlesbrough, was also exasperated. He said:

Agents must be controlled. The governing bodies have got to control their fees and the way they manipulate players. There have to be rules and regulations about the way they operate and the pay they receive. These agents want it all ways. They ask for a massive contract and if the player turns out to be top class they want more. But if the player underachieves he never takes a pay cut and the agent never knocks on the door offering a refund. The trouble is, clubs have paid inflated prices for ordinary players in the past and the agents have taken that as a yardstick.

Robson returned to the case of Jimmy Floyd Hasselbaink, Leeds' erstwhile striker. Hasselbaink had been told by his agent that he deserved a massive pay rise. When Leeds refused to give him one Hasselbaink made it clear that he would go, having been assured by his agent that Athletico Madrid would buy him and pay him what he wanted. Robson cited this as a classic example of what was happening in football:

Agents are going around saying, 'If you reach this price, I'll get him out' because they know the clubs will cave in. My sort of player, staying at a club all his life, is a thing of the past. It's not in the interests of the agents, even the quality ones, because the money is so vast. Soon no club will be able to hold on to a top-class player.

And it's going to be harder, the more clubs go around saying 'We want this player for £20 million and we don't care if he's under contract. Players are entitled to leave at the end of their contracts and all players deserve security against injury but they want a third clause too – the right to f— off with two years left if it suits them. And that's not on.

Even some agents were worried. Jon Holmes, who represented some of the biggest names in football, including Michael Owen and David Beckham, told club chairmen in summer 1999 that the authorities had to legislate to eliminate cowboy agents. He was especially concerned about agents who worked for clubs and players; an agent might try to unsettle a player at another club if he knew that another club was interested. He said that agents should be as highly qualified as accountants or lawyers: 'Without stronger legislation we will remain in the Wild West days of cowboy agents and we might as well abandon the whole licensing procedure as a bureaucratic irrelevance. That would leave footballers at the mercy of unscrupulous operators for a while but that is often the case now and it might solve the problem in the long run. The players would eventually see for themselves who are the agents most likely to take care of their interests.'

Chapter Nine

The Media

In the 1960s I devoured the work of the journalist who covered Brighton and Hove Albion for my local newspaper, the *Evening Argus*. I thought that he had the best job in the world. He travelled to exotic places, such as Barrow, Workington and Southport, and on Saturdays he occupied the front page of the *Argus* sports special with his staccato reports on Albion's endeavours that afternoon.

As a trainee journalist in Plymouth in the early 1970s I was similarly in awe of the reporter who followed Plymouth Argyle. He knew the manager, spoke to the players and saw every game, home and away. Then I moved to the London *Evening Standard* and had my first sight of major league football sports writers. They were middle aged or older and trekked around the country and Europe, following local giants such as Spurs, Chelsea and Arsenal. But the editor did not take much notice of sport, which occupied a few pages at the back of the newspaper, since what really mattered was hard news, Londoner's Diary – the page of snippets cataloguing the activities of the city's glitteratti – and the arts. Football only mattered – and on such occasions was moved to the front pages – when there was hooliganism, which confirmed the view of the middle classes who were the *Standard*'s core audience that the sport was played and watched by morons.

Late in 1979 I moved to *The Sunday Times*, first as a freelance and then as a reporter on staff. The sports pages were edited by John Lovesey, a charming and accomplished journalist. Despite the limitations imposed by ancient production techniques and grasping print unions, Lovesey demonstrated every week that sports journalism consisted of more than cliché-strewn match reports. He elevated sports photography to an art form. His star was Chris Smith, who planned his photographic coverage of a football match in advance, as if it was a military operation. Once, during the World Cup in Spain in 1982, Smith explained to me that he reconnoitred unfamiliar stadia to make sure that he picked the right spot; his weekly photographs, always gripping, often stunning, were the result of interpretation and anticipation, not of watching the ball.

Lovesey also assembled a team of first-class journalists led by Brian Glanville, the prolific novelist and fluent Italian speaker who could have been a successful literary critic. But Glanville lived for football and was one of the most respected commentators in the country. He was also player-manager of a park team called Chelsea Casuals, which he packed with young players. Most were far too good to be slogging through the mud of council pitches but Glanville's stature in the sport was such that they were flattered when he invited them to represent the Casuals. Everyone knew him; once I heard a team of louts discussing his demolition of an England full back in that morning's *Sunday Times*. He had already celebrated his fiftieth birthday and spent most games parked at full back, yelling instructions to his fit, mobile team. It was obvious that he had never been much of a player, but this did not matter; it was a joy to watch him because you knew that, in his head, he was playing for one of his beloved Italian clubs.

Meanwhile the sports team at the newspaper struggled for respectability. Arnold Wesker, the distinguished playwright, described them as fringe members of *The Sunday Times* in his book *Journey Into Journalism*, which chronicled two months at the newspaper in summer 1971. Wesker also said that the sports team felt guilty that they were not covering *important* events, like wars or famines. They were anxious to make it clear that they were not dummies: 'Sport is a fascist activity in that it's governed by rules against which there is no appeal and which, if applied to a democratic society, could not be upheld,' one unnamed sports hack pompously told Wesker.

Sport was still a minor department at *The Sunday Times* in 1982 when I was dispatched to Spain to cover the World Cup for news. (Every newspaper sent ordinary reporters, as well as football writers, in the expectation that English fans would run amok.) Football was not yet a global business, which was just as well since newspapers were technically – and financially – unable to give the tournament the massive coverage that recent World Cups have enjoyed.

I spent a pleasant few weeks pottering around Spain in search of non-existent English thugs. I watched the press with interest. The news reporters from the tabloids hunted in packs, elevating the handful of skirmishes involving English supporters into full-scale street battles, in between collecting blank receipts from restaurants.

The football writers were organised hierarchically. The quality press analysed soberly. The middle market had teams, led by the Number One, who reported England and wrote the major 'think pieces', followed by a Number Two and a Number Three, both of whom were careful never to outwrite – or outdress – the Number One. The tabloids had similar teams but they were operating under instructions from HQ; thus, each day brought fresh attacks on the manager or a player, interspersed with bogus revelations.

The massacre of Israeli athletes by Palestinian terrorists at the Munich Olympics in 1972 had forced new, and depressing, levels of security on the organisers of major sports tournaments. Now the media had to wear electronic tags, which graded individuals according to status; hence, a lowly hack from a British provincial newspaper would only be allowed into the press centre, while the BBC's star commentator could wander around the bowels of a stadium, chatting to managers and players.

But, even so, by today's standards the 1982 World Cup in Spain was relaxed. The Russian team flip-flopped around a package-tour hotel outside Marbella, along with the press. They swam in the pool, ate in the restaurant and flirted with women. Their coaches were extraordinarily friendly, although they were popularly supposed to be KGB officers. Once I was invited to join a practice session; tragically, I had to decline since I had hurt my knee a few weeks earlier playing for Battersea Park. After Scotland had been knocked out of the competition – by the Russians – I saw some of their players relaxing in the bars of a marina complex called Puerto Banus a few miles from Marbella, disappointed at their defeat but also relieved that they could now go home. None of this could happen today. Security – and fear of the press – would prevent players behaving like ordinary people.

My next overseas foray came the following year when *The Sunday Times* magazine sent me to Barcelona to report on Diego Maradona, who the club had just bought for the then staggering sum of £4.8 million. This was equivalent to £9.6 million in January 2000; Maradona would have been worth at least £25 million, and probably much more, if he was playing today. He was paid around half a million pounds in salary and bonuses. Today that would be about £1 million; ordinary Premier League players now earn over £1 million a year.

Maradona was the first multinational player; he was a billboard for companies and the star whose presence would ensure massive television audiences. He had the build of a weightlifter – the result of steroids fed to him by clubs in Argentina who wanted to supplement his speed with bulk and strength – and gabbled nonsense to the journalists who followed him everywhere. He was a semi-literate young man from the slum of Buenos Aires, who had unimaginable wealth and fame because he was one of the best players in the history of football. But at least he was protected from himself – he was already emerging as an addictive personality, who sought pleasure in drugs, booze and the sort of women who could be found selling their bodies in Argentinian back streets – by his manager, Jorge Cyterszpiler, a friend two years older than Maradona and many times more intelligent. Cyterszpiler had been crippled by polio as a boy, was middle class and well-educated, and yet the two were close, though the manager was indisputably the master; he indulged Maradona's weaknesses, but never to the extent that they threatened his fragile mental and physical health.

Barcelona was an unusual member of the elite of European clubs. It drew support from a region, Catalonia, rather than a city and symbolised a Catalan's aspirations for independence from the capital, Madrid. But in other ways it was a typical club; like Manchester United, Arsenal, Liverpool, Bayern Munich, Roma, Lazio, Napoli, Marseilles, the two Milans and so on it was a business which had to expand or wither. The Spanish leagues and cups were only valued by fans when they involved matches against Real Madrid; to generate the millions necessary to buy players the club had continually to excite the supporters. And this meant games against the legends of Europe.

It was the start of the revolution which led to UEFA's ersatz European Super League in the late 1990s, when the European Cup became the Champions' League. It also marked the beginning of the end for internationals; clubs did not want to risk their expensive commodities even for major competitions, such as the World Cup and the European Championship. Nor did the players care whether they represented their countries or not; once it had been an honour which could boost their club salaries but players were earning so much by the end of the century that many could not be bothered with internationals.

Newspapers had always been produced by journalists who belonged to the National Union of Journalists. They used typewriters and, if they were out of the office, filed their stories by dictating to them to copytakers. They were paid well but were not rich. There were few celebrity columnists or commentators because newspapers demanded that their regular contributors belonged to the NUJ. This was also the pre-celebrity, pre-*Hello!* era of the 1970s and early 1980s; people were well-known because they did something, not because the media required a pool of 'famous' people to interview.

175

The press relied on the printers, whose unions were so greedy that they made the NUJ seem feeble. The elite were the compositors, highly skilled men (there were no women) who translated words and pictures into slabs of hot metal, using machines that had been consigned to museums elsewhere in the developed world. Many printers were decent men but others were not; for them newspapers were cash dispensers. The abuses were legion – phantom men were paid and their wages divided amongst the real workers, and extra payments were regularly demanded on Saturday nights, just as the presses were scheduled to roll, because the building was too hot or too cold, or because the printers had 'discovered' that the front page story was a minute late – and it could not go on.

In 1986 Rupert Murdoch demolished the unions when he moved his newspapers to Wapping. Other newspapers soon followed. Editors could now order a new section on the arts, leisure, property or sport without worrying about the unions. By the end of the 1980s, therefore, the press was in a position to report, and fuel, the revolution that turned football into a glamorous industry.

The British media had begun its reassessment of football – as an industry that should have been scrapped along with the mills and shipyards – a year earlier, in May 1985, after the disasters at Bradford City and the Heysel in Brussels. In the following months there were many articles by distinguished writers, most of whom had never been to a football match, about what it all meant. The more liberal, and thoughtful, concluded that, while Thatcherism had destroyed much that was bad, it had also isolated too many people; they were the dispossessed, who felt loyalty only to their mates on the terraces.

Football, however, learnt nothing from these tragedies. Clubs continued to be run like medieval fiefdoms by directors who gloried in their status; managers gibbered nonsense, and players demanded ever-increasing amounts of money from clubs. The fans were treated with contempt; football knew that they would always be there, packed on terraces in the wind and rain, munching overpriced hot dogs and relieving themselves in overflowing toilets. Then came the carnage at Hillsborough in 1989.

Hillsborough was such a catastrophe that it could not be forgotten, as Bradford and Heysel had been. It was a good story; it had death, victims and villains but, most important, it had the twists of a conspiracy. Stories are not judged by their intrinsic importance – every day awful things happen around the world which are ignored or summed up in a paragraph by newspapers – but by whether they possess a special drama which will appeal to readers and viewers. Local participation in a story – British victims or British heroes – is a major plus. Children and animals often propel an event into the headlines. And conspiracy always interests the media, because it generates excitement. Hillsborough had this last, vital ingredient. While Lord Justice Taylor prepared his report into the disaster the media discovered that the real culprit was football itself. Football was now being examined by tough, independent journalists, not by football writers, many of whom did not have the ability to piece together the financial, social and historical strands which were the background to Hillsborough.

Taylor's was the ninth official report on football since 1900 and few believed that it would achieve much. Football was doomed. Many journalists thought that this was a shame since the game had bound together communities and shown that Thatcher had been wrong to argue that society consisted only of self-interested individuals.

It took the World Cup in Italy in 1990, to prove that football had evolved from a relic of a vanished country, to a bright new business.

I was dispatched to Sardinia, England's base for the opening three matches, by the *Sunday Correspondent*. This was where England had been dumped by FIFA, in what amounted to quarantine, in the hope that England would fail to qualify for the later rounds.

Once again, the news reporters from the tabloids were there, hunting in packs for violent fans and blank receipts. As always, they portrayed the little outbreaks of violence, of the sort seen in city centres throughout Britain after closing time every Saturday night, as if war had broken out. Most English supporters were staying in hotels and treated this as a summer holiday and while the few hundred fans who fitted the hooligan stereotype were ugly they were not dangerous; they wandered around the scruffy capital, Cagliari, and the rest of this rugged island, chanting and trying to look tough, but no one took them seriously. At night they could be found on benches, beaches or in makeshift camp sites, snoring off the effects of too much cheap wine and sun. After a few days even the police, who had been looking forward to testing themselves against psychotic hordes, were bored at the lack of action.

But the tabloid reporters had a job to do and expenses to justify and so they wrote stories about crazed English thugs terrorising the island and, when the absence of serious injuries or arrests made it impossible to sustain this fantasy, they switched to bashing the Italian police, who, they screamed, were brutal, like all foreigners.

The football writers, meanwhile, indignant that they were marooned here, while the rest of the world was enjoying the real World Cup on the mainland savaged England's manager, the lugubrious but decent Bobby Robson for his caution and lack of vision; they said that a few players, were talented but gutless, like John Barnes and Chris Waddle, while most had spirit but no ability. The broadsheet press put it elegantly; the middle market tabloids were more acerbic but still rational; the mass-market tabloids were simply abusive.

Football in England had reached the decisive moment. The World Cup proper, as compared with the dreary little tournament in Sardinia, was bubbling along nicely, but was not a classic; there were no great teams, like the old Brazil, and no outstanding players. (Maradona was a preposterous, bloated figure, who spent most of his time falling over and complaining.) There were interesting developments, such as the emergence of Cameroon, but the romance of this was spoilt by the fact that, unlike previous surprise teams in the World Cup, such as the North Koreans in

1966, most of the Africans representing Cameroon were already playing for European teams.

England slogged their way through games against the Republic of Ireland, Holland and Egypt and qualified for the next round, in Bologna against Belgium. The Scots went home but the Irish moved to Genoa to face Romania. Sardinia had been a non-event and there was general relief that we were leaving, but no one expected to remain on the mainland for long.

Then England beat the Belgians in a thrilling match. We moved to Naples, the maddest, most corrupt city in Europe, and squeezed past Cameroon. The tabloid news reporters were irrelevant now; back home their editors were being swept up in a frenzy of excitement as the impossible – England playing in a World Cup Final – became possible. Hence, these reporters scratched around, writing captions for photographs of English fans who had pawned everything to be here, while grumbling to each other about the good old days of hooliganism and players in three-in-a-bed romps with local girls. There was also a new icon, Paul Gascoigne, a buffoon off the field but a genius on it.

The semi-final in Turin against West Germany signalled the birth of the new football. There were unforgettable moments, notably when Gascoigne started to cry when he realised that a booking meant he would miss the final and Gary Lineker signalled his concern to Robson. England lost on a penalty shoot-out but that did not matter. In England the streets were deserted as tens of millions, many of whom had always loathed football, watched the game on television. Television and the press realised that, providing it was packaged properly, football could now appeal to the A/B social groups and to women. This was exciting because these were precisely the people whom advertisers targeted. It was also exciting because football could fill up so much space and air time cheaply; it was a continuous event which was always taking place, unlike real news, which was messy and unpredictable. Britain was small, uneventful and law-abiding and foreign news

179

was wars, sundry natural disasters and politicians with unpro-
nounceable names. Football was the salvation: it was show
business with attitude.

Newspapers expanded their sports sections. The Sunday press
fought back, with ever-thicker sports pages. The daily newspapers
replied with supplements on Saturdays and Mondays. Football
writers became superstars, were paid handsomely and were often
the subject of transfer rumours, like the players whom they wrote
about. The demarcation lines between quality, middle market and
tabloids became blurred because these acres of newsprint could no
longer be filled with vacuous gossip. As football became a
multibillion pound industry, newspapers required journalists with
different skills; football writers on the broadsheets had always been
accomplished writers while the tabloids had demanded polemicists
or hacks who could find – or manufacture – 'exclusives' with the
help of a cheque book. The tabloids had also padded out their
football pages with ghosted columns by star managers and players.
    The standard of football coverage rose. The broadsheets
analysed football's finances, the competence of the sport's administrators and the impact of the foreign invasion. The middle-market
tabloids faced a more difficult task; they required sensation but, on
the other hand, their audience was almost as sophisticated as the
broadsheets'. They needed football to boost circulation but they
also had to be critical. Thus, on a typical day they would run an
interview with a leading manager, who bemoaned the greed of the
star foreigners, a profile of an unsettled Frenchman at Arsenal, who
complained about the aggression of the game here, a double-page
spread describing how football was killing the lower division clubs
and an attack by a columnist on the damage caused by clubs
becoming limited companies. Meanwhile, the mass-market tabloids
still ran sensationalised rubbish, as they always had done, but they
also hired journalists who could write as intelligently as their
colleagues on other newspapers.
    'Celebrities' also clambered aboard. The weekend newspapers

were stuffed with columns by politicians, disc jockeys, actors (and actresses) and pop novelists, all of whom claimed to be lifelong football fanatics. But football was cool and was a vital part of a celebrity's public persona.

Until now football literature had been relatively sparse. Other sports, notably cricket, had spawned wonderful books but football had had to make do with solid reportage. *The Glory Game* and *Only a Game?* were the best of a not very large bunch.

The first sign that football was now a subject for serious writers came with the publication in 1990 of *All Played Out*, an hilarious account of the 1990 World Cup by Pete Davies. Two years later came Nick Hornby and *Fever Pitch*. By the late 1990s the publishing industry was churning out well-written, provocative books about the game, many of which were collaborations between players and journalists. There were still many worthless books, with pap titles such as *My Story So Far*, the account of the life of a twenty-two-year-old Premier League player with one England cap, or *Hitting The Net*, but others were first-rate. With the aid of Hugh McIlvanney, one of the country's most distinguished sports writers, Sir Alex Ferguson produced a gripping autobiography.

Meanwhile the relationship between journalists and players changed fundamentally over the years. In the era of the maximum wage players had been humble workers, often earning less than the reporters who interviewed them. They were respectful of these men (there were no women football writers then) with notebooks who had good, steady jobs which did not depend on the state of their knees or ankles. Their attitude reflected a class-conscious society; reporters were middle class and had to be deferred to. The civilised relationship between the two camps was also possible because the media was smaller and less intrusive. National newspapers carried match reports, analysis and interviews, but, compared with the coverage of the 1990s, it was sparse and restrained. Regional and local newspapers assigned reporters to clubs, who became trusted members of the organisations. Unlike players and managers, who came and went, these journalists were permanent fixtures. A club was part of the community, and had to be reported honestly, but there was much that should remain private; hence, the reporter who covered City, United or Rovers would not dream of revealing that the star centre forward was a drunk or that the goalkeeper spent every night at the dog stadium. These were family matters, to be resolved internally. By the 1970s players were earning substantial amounts, which bred a new confidence. But they still had the same worries as the fans, about the mortgage, the new sofa which the wife wanted and the crunch from their gearbox when they accelerated. Hence, the Spurs players of the early 1970s were both open and deferential to Hunter Davies when he was researching *The Glory Game*; he worked for posh papers and had it made.

The growth of the media and the explosion of players' wages changed everything. There were more newspapers with more space to fill. Once a star writer, such as Brian Glanville, could destroy a player's reputation with a stinging column but now there were dozens of pundits competing for the readers' attention and none could exert a decisive influence.

The gulf between press and players widened during the 1980s, even in the lower divisions. Although players' wages here remained modest they did not trust the press any more than their colleagues in the First Division because they knew that journalists were only interested in scandals.

The 1990s saw a new relationship. Satellite television turned Premier League players into multimillionaires. These young men regarded most journalists as losers who earned a few thousand quid a year and drove poky cars. There were now so many reporters, from newspapers, magazines, radio and television, begging for interviews that players could pick and choose who they talked to. There were a few superstar writers, such as McIlvanney, who were treated respectfully but the top players were, at best, dismissive of rank and file reporters and, at worst, downright contemptuous. Players were more sophisticated; they knew what the press wanted and had no intention of giving it to them, unless they were paid large amounts. But usually their agents advised them to hang on to their revelations until they were close to retirement, when they could dictate their memories to a ghost writer to turn into a bestselling book.

The main beneficiaries of football's transformation into the new show business worked in television. Once football on television had consisted of a commentator who was never seen and a man in a sports jacket with a moustache sitting in a studio, with a teleprinter clattering out the results. But now these men, and an increasing number of women, usually young, pretty and slinky, became superstars.

Sport, particularly football, was the main weapon in the armoury of the free terrestrial stations, BBC and ITV, the satellite, digital and cable companies. To attract viewers these stations competed fiercely with each other for the rights to show football. But acquiring matches was only the beginning; apart from technical gimmicks, they needed to turn presenters, pundits and commentators into personalities.

The first was an amiable, middle-aged man with a talent for self-deprecation, called Des Lynam. He had risen steadily and unspectacularly through the BBC's sporting ranks and, by the 1990 World Cup, had established himself as the corporation's number one sports presenter. In the past these men, like David Coleman, had been far less valued than, say, news readers and had earned modest salaries but that changed now. Lynam *became* the World Cup. The BBC and ITV poured millions into their coverage, vying for the slickest studio sets, the most entertaining pundits and the most controversial analysis. Thanks to Lynam, who managed to be all things – avuncular, cheeky, funny, passionate, aloof and, remarkably, a sex symbol – the BBC won easily. Then BSkyB bought the new Premier League and began to squeeze the BBC – and, to a lesser extent, ITV – out of football. BSkyB needed anchor people, commentators and pundits and was prepared to pay Premier League-style salaries to acquire them. Ex-players, such as Andy Gray, were recruited, experienced performers were lured from the terrestrial stations and new talent found, usually attractive young women whose presence on screen guaranteed that men would tune in.

As more football was broadcast it became increasingly tricky to convince audiences that games were special. It had been easy at first because live matches had been a novelty but by the mid-1990s viewers were tired of being told that a midweek evening match between two mid-table Premier League teams was the sports event of the year. Sometimes the matches turned out to be better than expected but usually they were what they were: ordinary games which no one would have bothered televising a few years earlier. But television could not say this because it needed to maintain the illusion that football was qualitatively better than it had ever been.

Privately, men like Lynam knew that this was silly but they could not say so because they had become rich through football. Only veterans reaching the end of their careers, such as Ron Atkinson, the ex-manager, could tell the truth; he often told ITV viewers that games were 'rubbish', which suggested that his television career would end shortly.

The reaction in August 1999 to the news that Des Lynam, then fifty-five years old, was joining ITV demonstrated that these men and women were now national celebrities. The tabloid press screamed that 'the BBC is in crisis as Des quits'when he left the corporation to become ITV's anchorman on a four-year deal worth £5 million. His defection was followed by a series of stories speculating on the identity of his successor – as if the host of a football programmes on the BBC was the broadcasting equivalent of becoming Pope, and investigations into what had gone wrong at the BBC, as if, somehow, the corporation should have matched ITV's offer.

After much debate Gary Lineker, the ex-England striker who always looked as if he had just had a bath, took over from Lynam. He had two regular assistants: Trevor Brooking and Alan Hansen, ex-Liverpool and Scotland. Brooking was a successful business-man and sports administrator who looked as if he had been time-warped from the BBC of the 1960s. So, too, were the BBC stalwart commentators, Barry Davies and John Motson, whom viewers knew were wrapped up in sheepskin coats and sensible scarves as they commentated on matches. But Hansen was definitely 1990s.

He was clipped and rude. Like Lynam he was often profiled by the press, who said that, actually, he was a nice chap whose abruptness masked insecurity. He did not pretend that pontificating on television had been an ambition; he had been a marvellous player but, alas, had just missed the wage explosion which would have allowed a prosperous retirement. He had quit in 1991 after seventeen seasons, and eight championship medals, on a salary of about £3,000 a week (about £3,700 in 2000); if he had been playing today he would be earning at least £35,000 a week.

For newspapers and television football's explosion into a global industry has been marvellous for business; it has also been good news for journalists, ex-players and managers, middle-aged men with moustaches and young women with good figures who know that 4-4-2 is not the name of the latest girl band. But if football implodes, many of these people will be looking for alternative employment.

Chapter Ten

The Future is Now

It is the new millennium and the future is here. A few years ago I explained to a friend how I thought football would evolve. Television viewers would be able to track a player around the pitch. After fans became bored with that, gimmick, tiny cameras and microphones would be fixed to players' shirts so that they could *be* them. Next there would be uncensored coverage of managers screaming abuse from the touchline dugouts. Television would invade the dressing rooms so that viewers could watch managers cursing their players. Television would have to do this to give the impression that football was becoming more exciting. And all this would cost extra. No, said my friend, people aren't stupid. They won't pay.

In summer 1999 Sky launched an interactive service. This allowed viewers to replay incidents, select camera angles and call up data, such as how many times a player had touched the ball. In the New Year Sky refined the service. Now viewers could track a player. By stabbing your remote control, and adding a few pounds to your Sky bill, you could study David Beckham as he flicked his hair, scratched his designer stubble and tied up his bootlaces. Soon you will be able to sit in your living room and *be* on a pitch, thanks to three-dimensional television.

These developments are taking place because television believes that sport, notably football, is the key to attracting viewers. But they must repackage the game constantly to titillate the public.

Only the biggest clubs benefit because television is not interested in the second-rate. Small clubs are so desperate to reach the Premiership that they buy players whom they cannot afford. The few that are promoted are immediately relegated, with insupportable debts. But the Premier League rolls on.

A map of England shows why this madness cannot continue. Most of the twenty Premier League clubs and the seventy-two clubs of the Nationwide League are in decaying inner cities and towns where the factories and mines have long closed. London is unique because it is so wealthy, with an economy almost as big as Switzerland's; the major clubs here – Spurs, Arsenal and Chelsea – have become leisure–entertainment–lifestyle corporations. West Ham are comfortable. Charlton bounce back and forth between the Premier League and the First Division, husbanding their resources so that they can survive regular relegation. Fulham have a megarich patron, the eccentric Mohammed al Fayed.

But other London clubs are struggling. Wimbledon might perish after being relegated from the Premiership. Crystal Palace almost went bankrupt. Queen's Park Rangers, Millwall, Leyton Orient and Brentford were once in the First Division; it will be a miracle if all are full-time professional clubs by the end of the next decade. Barnet simply exist. In other major cities there are a few giants, notably Manchester United, Leeds United and Liverpool, who have also become international brand names, but others are limping along. Newcastle United are £72 million in debt; Middlesbrough have discovered that money does not guarantee success; Sheffield Wednesday have sold their best players to try and balance the books but are now in the First Division. Analysts in the City are predicting that the unthinkable will happen soon: a major club will go bankrupt. In the First Division once-mighty clubs, such as Birmingham, Wolves and Portsmouth, pray that the Premier League will form a Premier League Division Two so that they can share in the bonanza. Below them are dozens of clubs for whom daily survival is a triumph. In Europe a handful of clubs dominate in each country. Spain has Barcelona and Real Madrid. In France there is Marseilles, Bordeaux, Monaco and Paris Saint-Germain. Portugal has Benfica, Sporting Lisbon and Porto. Holland has Ajax, PSV Eindhoven and Feyenoord. The well-organised Germans have more, including Bayern Munich, Borussia Dortmund, Hertha Berlin and Leverkusen. Serie A in Italy is packed with legendary clubs. This is testimony to the Italians' passion for the game, their fierce local pride and the fact that clubs are traditionally backed by billionaire industrialists. Here we have AC and Inter Milan, Lazio, Fiorentina, Parma, Juventus, Roma and the rest. Throughout Europe pay-per-view television is common, providing the major clubs with tens of millions of pounds a year. Usually there is another national division but beneath that there are semi-professional and amateur regional leagues.

England, however, clings to ninety-two professional clubs. Football has always been pragmatic yet, paradoxically, it is also romantic; it does not want to abandon these relics of a vanished society, clustered around towns which lost their *raison d'être* many years ago. But finance has no emotion and there are many clubs in the First, Second and Third Divisions that need urgent help from television, the Premier League, local government and business.

It would be a pity if they folded. A football club is a focus in an age when communities have broken down. It offers escape for youngsters from the couch potato, virtual reality of television and the Internet; a local club is about real people, not multimillionaire 'celebrities'. Many small clubs, such as Watford, Leyton Orient and Millwall, are striving to convince locals that they are more than football teams. They believe that they can save boys – and girls – from drugs, crime and despair and they are right. But they need money to do this.

Violence always simmers in football, whether it is played by pub teams in parks, where goalposts wobble and nets are only used for cup finals, or at Old Trafford before 60,000 fans and tens of millions of television and Internet viewers. But referees are abused today in a manner which would have been unthinkable in the past because many young people despise authority in any form, whether it is a policeman, a traffic warden, a teacher or a bloke in a black strip with a whistle.

They take their lead from today's Premiership stars. Many of these young men have the arrogance that comes from wealth. They believe that they are above the rules of the game; some even think that they are above the law.

The richer the player the worse he behaves. The journeymen of the lower divisions cannot afford to be fined by their clubs or the FA for indiscipline but these penalties are meaningless to Premiership players. And absence of fear breeds anarchy.

Stroll around London and examine the blue plaques on the façades of houses where the famous of other ages once lived; on them you will find the names of artists, writers, actors, musicians and scientists. Today many of these kinds of people live in grotty houses in the suburbs. Money is the barometer of success and the people who have lots of it – City hustlers, Internet entrepreneurs, television presenters and Premiership footballers – are icons for the young. When a player runs to the referee, snarling and screaming abuse, he must be right because he is a millionaire and the ref is a self-employed electrician. The young absorb this: if you have loads of money you can do what you like.

Early in 2000 the millionaire players of Manchester United demonstrated their contempt for authority when they protested, harangued and generally tried to bully referees. United were not a dirty team: statistics showed that they had committed the fewest fouls in that season's Premiership. The problem was their attitude towards authority. Against Middlesbrough one football reporter said that 'a lynch mob' of United players had surrounded the referee to protest against a penalty. Alex Ferguson admitted that behaviour like this was 'out of order' but a fortnight later, at St James' Park in Newcastle, his players spent much of the game chasing the referee. Once the huge Dutch defender Jaap Stam thrust his shaven head within inches of an assistant referee, as if he was going to butt him.

As United's valuation on the Stock Exchange soared to over £800 million – putting them within a couple of hundred million of becoming the world's first billion pound football club – Ferguson grumbled that there was 'a vendetta' against United because they were so successful. He said:

> We're getting criticised for protesting, yet it is wrong to victimise Manchester United when the whole country is the same. Players argue every decision. It's not just Manchester United. Our players are going to have to be perfect in their behaviour to keep the hounds at bay because one blemish and we're slaughtered. It's too easy to say that because we're Manchester United we deserve this. These players have every right to earn a living the same as other players. Because they're better than most at it doesn't mean they should be judged worse than others. But that is what is happening. We've had to face that for years but what the players are finding very strange is that since we won the European Cup the hatred has got more.

This was nonsense. It was like saying an Oscar-winning actor in a Porsche can spit at the policeman who pulls him over to take a breath test because he thinks that the policeman has singled him out because he is famous. It is not difficult to imagine the reaction of youngsters: if United treat officials like this it must be okay, mustn't it?

In the weeks after these unsavoury events there were signs that young players were indeed aping the Premier League stars. Malcolm Berry, chief executive of the English Schools FA, said that 'the wrong example is being set at the top'. He continued, 'For anyone to suggest otherwise is ludicrous. It's a well-known fact that young players copy their role models who play for Manchester United, Chelsea, Arsenal or whoever.' Nottingham Forest's youth director, Paul Hart, was also worried: 'I can understand players getting frustrated but there has to be self-control. Young players watch more and more football on television and they are vulnerable to what they see.'

The organisation that benefited from this demonstration of Premiership arrogance was the Football Association. Since the formation of that division in 1992 the FA had been searching for a role. The elite were independent in practice if not legally, while the seventy-two clubs of the Football League brooded about the injustice of the Premier League and blamed the FA for letting it happen. This was Adam Crozier's opportunity to show that the FA was the only organisation in football capable of distinguishing between right and wrong. He said that the FA would not allow the millionaires of the Premiership to destroy the game. Four clubs – Leeds and Spurs, Chelsea and Wimbledon, who had just behaved like lager louts in Majorca – were charged with bringing the game into disrepute and Crozier warned the rest that the FA would protect officials from the kind of verbal and physical intimidation which was becoming common. In late March 2000 the FA fined Leeds and Spurs £150,000 each and warned clubs generally that the Association would not tolerate a repeat of this kind of disgraceful behaviour. It was vital, said the FA, that players recognised that they were 'role models' who had a duty to young fans, which was an admirable but somewhat belated sentiment from an organisation which, frankly, had always been more interested in its own survival.

There are 33,000 referees in England but only a handful in the Premiership and Nationwide League. Premiership refs are paid £600 per match and their assistants £225; Nationwide officials receive £195 and £95. They have to retire when they are forty-eight. Every referee has to start at the bottom, on park pitches, where violence against referees by players with a grudge against the world is common. In the 1998–9 season, two hundred and sixty-four referees were attacked. Youngsters have always aped the stars. (When Denis Law was at his peak every young player used to hold his shirt cuffs at the wrists, just like the maestro.) Now they are spitting at each other, diving as soon as an opponent comes near them and surrounding referees if they don't like a decision – all of which they see every week on television.

It takes at least six years to reach the two major professional leagues, a tiring ascent through the amateur and semi-professional game, where there is no glory and no money. Managers often accuse top referees of making dramatic decisions because they want to be noticed; perhaps this is occasionally true but it is ridiculous to suggest that a referee in the Premiership set out to be famous when he (or she) first stepped out with a whistle on to a park pitch.

The debate over referees is as old as football. There have been many ideas to eliminate human error, such as instant video replays or dividing the pitch into two halves, each patrolled by a referee. But video evidence is not always conclusive; England's third goal in the 1966 World Cup Final, when Geoff Hurst's shot hit the underside of the bar and bounced on the line, has been analysed countless times using computers but we still do not know whether the linesman, Tofik Bahkramov, from Russia, was right. *Match of the Day* once spent five minutes trying to establish whether a player was offside but, despite numerous cameras, behind the goal, on both sides of the ground and high above it, no one could be sure. An experiment with two referees was also not a success; everything went smoothly when the ball was inside a half but both officials blew their whistles when it bobbled around the centre circle.

Full-time referees are not a solution either. Refereeing is a hobby, not a career, which attracts men and women from all social backgrounds. Would the authorities recruit potential full-time referees, as if they were trainee accountants? Would successful candidates be guaranteed jobs as full-time referees? Could they be sacked for incompetence? How would the thousands of men and women who dream of joining the league list react to being told that they have no chance of trotting out at Old Trafford or Anfield? The Premiership could afford to employ full-time referees but the First,

Second and Third Division clubs could not. Nationwide referees are often promoted to the elite division – and poor ones relegated from the Premiership – but that could not happen if the Premiership had its own full-time officials. Professional referees might be fitter but would still make mistakes.

Philip Don, a former headmaster and FIFA referee who is the Premiership's referees officer, said that it was futile to search for perfection. 'We have the best referees in the world but they are human. The problem is that football reflects society and there are less people in authority today who are treated with the same respect as they were when I was a boy.'

Another veteran referee, Keith Hackett, said that changes in the laws of the game, the influx of foreign players, many of whom come from countries where acting is part of the game, and the amount of money at stake, had put referees under intolerable pressure. 'Tackling has almost been taken away altogether. That has put a fear in defenders, causing a huge increase in shirt-pulling. And there is no doubt players are going to ground when they have not been touched and that is because of the foreign influence.'

Steve Baines was the only ex-professional player in 2000 amongst the Nationwide League's fifty-two referees and two hundred and eighteen assistant referees. With only three seasons to go before compulsory retirement, Baines was unlikely to realise his dream of taking charge of a game at one of the country's great stadia. His critics said that he had found it difficult to make the transition from playing to refereeing; sometimes he ignored gamesmanship, such as sides retreating very slowly at free kicks, because he regarded this as part of the game, while a referee who had never played professionally punished this as cheating.

Baines only started refereeing after he retired as a player because he thought that it would help him find a job in management. He had joined Nottingham Forest, then in the First Division, as an apprentice on £5 a week in 1969. He was a solid, hard-working centre half and had a steady career, mostly in the lower divisions; after Forest he went to Huddersfield, Bradford City, Walsall and

Bury before moving to Scunthorpe as player-coach. He spent two seasons at Chesterfield as player-coach and helped them win promotion from the Fourth Division in 1986 but slipped out of football after that, the victim, he said, of 'boardroom politics'.

He already had a coaching qualification from the FA and decided that he would add to his portfolio of skills by becoming a referee. He began with Sunday games in parks and slowly edged his way up, through amateur and semi-professional leagues, until he became an assistant referee five years later with the Football League (the Nationwide became sponsors in August 1996) and a referee the following year.

Like other referees Baines was not doing this for money or glory; but he was unique because football had once been his profession. He said that he loved refereeing, though the schedule was gruelling. He had just driven to Brighton for a Third Division game, a round trip of almost five hundred miles. Next was Cheltenham, then Barnet and Cardiff. But it was worth it. 'You need to know the laws. But you also need a good sense of humour and you must know about man management,' he said.

Meanwhile, we saw what happens when not very bright young men are given too much money and adulation. Paul Gascoigne, whose tears during the 1990 World Cup semi-final against West Germany had started the football revolution, was carried off the pitch at Middlesbrough with a shattered arm and into oblivion. Gascoigne was thirty-two and his body could no longer obey instructions from his brain and, like a child, he had lashed out in frustration. His left arm had cracked into the forehead of a player from Aston Villa, but it was Gascoigne who was seriously injured. The FA charged him with misconduct but everyone knew that he had already suffered enough; he had been one of the most extraordinary talents in post-war football but had lacked the intelligence to deal with the money and fame. He had never fully recovered from a knee injury sustained in 1991 as a Spurs player when he chopped down Nottingham Forest's Gary Charles in the FA Cup Final. Since then he had lurched from crisis to crisis. He was always surrounded by fellow Geordies, who thought that good ol' Gazza only needed a few more jars of ale to perk him up.

Another victim was Stan Collymore, who should have been one of the world's leading strikers in 2000, as he neared his thirtieth birthday. Instead, since the mid-1990s he had hardly kicked a ball. He had spent his time beating up girlfriends and attending clinics to be treated for depression and assorted addictions. Meanwhile, to the fury of fans, he had collected £20,000 every week. Managers at Nottingham Forest, Liverpool, Aston Villa and Fulham had tried everything – sympathy, encouragement and tough talking – but all had been glad when he had moved on. Now, in the twilight of his career, he had been given a final chance by Leicester's manager, Martin O'Neill.

Unfortunately Collymore was determined to prove that he was a real man, and not a woman-bashing depressive. During a break in Spain, designed to 'bond' the Leicester team, he let off a fire extinguisher in a bar in a hotel, to show his team-mates that he was a good bloke. It did not have the desired effect. The team was thrown out of the hotel and recalled to England by O'Neill.

Unlike some managers in the Premiership, O'Neill realised that the football bubble would burst if players continued to ignore the standards of common decency. So he fined Collymore two weeks' wages – reported to total £32,000 – and warned him that he was on 'a yellow card'; he made it clear that Collymore would be fired if he caused the club more embarrassment. He also ordered him to do 'community duties' – including spending time with a teenager who had a brain tumour – in an attempt to persuade the player that he was fortunate to be fit and wealthy. But Collymore, babbled that he had 'just been having fun with the lads', and he 'hadn't killed anybody' and that he was only trying to enjoy 'the best years' of his life.

But the most important development in the first months of the new millennium involved money. The year began with First Division

Swindon, losing an estimated £25,000 a week, sacking the assistant manager and fourteen backroom staff. The club also sold two players for a mere £200,000 so that it could pay pressing bills. But this was forgotten immediately since Manchester United were considering sponsorship offers from global corporations.

Football was now such big business that *The Financial Times* ran a story on the candidates that wanted to replace Sharp, the Japanese electronics company whose name had been on United's shirts for the past eighteen years. The *FT* said that the front runners were computer and Internet giants, including Bill Gates' Mircosoft and Amazon, the online booksellers. United had toyed with the idea of a four-year deal worth £30 million with Emirates, the Middle East airline, but the *FT* speculated, correctly, that United wanted more from sponsorship than a straightforward fee.

The deal which United signed with Vodafone, the world's 'largest mobile phone service provider', was worth £30 million over 4 years. But Vodafone was not only going to appear as a logo on United's shirts; it would also provide what was called 'wireless Internet services' to United's estimated 12 million fans in Britain and abroad. In layman's language this meant that Vodafone intended to use its new generation of mobile phones as miniaturised televisions and computers. Thanks to the new WAP, or wireless application protocol, these phones would allow a fan on the beach in the Canaries to watch a United match, with commentaries in a dozen languages, or order replica shirts through the club's web site while travelling on a train to work.

This is a variation of *The Truman Show*, the film starring Jim Carrey as a man whose life is a twenty-four-hours-a-day television programme. The major clubs and the communications giants want to make us slaves to our portable phone-television-computers. We will always be watching and buying, and real life, and real football, will be something that people used to do. Other elite English clubs, such as Arsenal, Chelsea and Liverpool, are certain to follow United, since Vodafone's rivals know that football sells. 'Sport is something you must have if you want to drive up sales,' said Jean-

Paul de la Fuente, managing director of Media Content, a sports media consultancy. 'In terms of time and what people spend their money on, sport is the most important part of many people's lives.'

The Vodafone–United deal was signed as the Premier League pored over the next contract with television. A spokesman said that the new deal which would replace the existing contract with Sky and the BBC, signed in 1996 and worth £743 million over four years, would obviously have to take into account 'the new technology' – which was a way of saying that clubs were determined to make even more money.

First, there was the main television contract to broadcast a specified number of live matches. Next, there would be subsidiary deals for highlights. The Premiership was also toying with the idea of selling a second tier of live matches, perhaps to Sky's rival, the American cable company NTL, now backed by Microsoft, which could be screened on different days. No one cared that this would destroy the tradition of Saturday football.

The most popular clubs also wanted to launch their own pay-per-view stations, to show matches which terrestrial, satellite and cable television did not want. Finally, regional terrestrial television was preparing to bid for the rights to local Premiership teams.

The Premier League thought that it would make between £1 billion to £2 billion over four years, most of which would go to the twenty clubs, though it claimed that it would 'share' some money with the unfortunates in the Nationwide League to ensure that the 'wealth gap' did not widen further. But no one was fooled by this; the Premier League only worried about itself and it had not suddenly discovered a moral purpose.

It is past midnight and ITV has just shown the highlights of the top-of-the-table First Division match between Charlton and Fulham. It has been a dour game, of endeavour but little skill. Charlton are a fast, muscular team and, barring disaster, will be promoted. But unless they have £20 million or so to spend on players they will be lucky to last one season in the Premiership. A decent player costs a couple of million pounds today; you have to pay much more for one who could be a Premiership star. Nonetheless, the only difference between this match and one involving Premiership also-rans is the absence of hype and an interactive facility. Afterwards I pop out to a twenty-four-hour supermarket to buy milk. There, staring out at me from the magazine rack, are David Beckham and Posh Spice, draped around each other on the cover of *Hello!*. These photographs appeared six months earlier in *Vanity Fair*, but *Hello!* has calculated that few of its readers will have seen them and, even if they have, it does not matter because Posh and Becks are the new royalty. And whoever tired of seeing photographs of the late Diana, Princess of Wales?

The caption on the cover, above the photograph of them lying by a stream, Beckham bare-chested as usual, coos: 'VICTORIA AND DAVID BECKHAM: An intimate portrait of the golden couple'. Inside, accompanying more photographs of Posh and her semi-naked husband, is drivel which is sycophantic even by the standards of *Hello!*, a magazine that takes pride in fawning, anti-journalism. Gosh, the magazine says, aren't they gorgeous, beautiful, in blissful love and so, so successful.

> They are the ultimate couple who have it all. With a trendy penthouse flat near Manchester, just a short drive from David's 'office', and an enormous mock-Georgian mansion within spitting distance of London (and Victoria's parents, so should the Beckhams fancy a romantic *diner à deux* at the Ivy restaurant Brooklyn (their baby son) can be looked after by his doting granny), a garage full of expensive motors and more diamonds than the de Beers vaults, the two demonstrate their wealth – rumoured to be anything between £18 million and £25 million – with style and panache.

Next morning Posh is front page news again after her appearance as a model at a fashion show in London. She has been photographed in a variety of outfits which reveal that she has a firm upper body and the legs of a marathon runner. Her fellow-models, however, had not been able to study her physique; while they changed in a dressing room, Posh had been allocated a cubicle to ensure her privacy.

A few days later there is more on Beckham. 'Friends' – which is the media's code for his agents and spin doctors – say that he has been reconciled with Ferguson. They say that he never wanted to leave United and will be signing a new contract worth, oh, about £60,000 a week, thus emphasising that he, not Roy Keane, the captain, is the real star of the team. But doubts grow about how good he really is. In yet another European match – against Fiorentina of Italy – Keane tackles ferociously and scores a goal of stupendous power and Ryan Giggs slides past defenders as if they are embedded in concrete, but Beckham is a peripheral figure. He passes neatly but his famed crosses and free kicks do not trouble Fiorentina's goalkeeper and, as usual, he tackles like a petulant child. Beckham seems to realise that he is a footballer, not a model, and the following Saturday he trots out against Leicester sporting a Keane-style shaven head; as if saying to himself, his manager and his nagging wife that he is going to get stuck in and prove that he is as good as his publicity machine claims.

It is fitting that the third millennium opened with Posh and Becks because football has become a branch of showbusiness. Celebrities like them are the main weapons in the battle between the new technology multinationals. It would be silly to blame Posh and Becks for taking advantage of this; we would all like to be famous and rich, even if we knew that we did not deserve to be. But football should remember why it became the world's favourite game. If it is not careful it will soon be a victim of its own greed. First to go will be the sponsors who will not want to be associated with foul-mouthed louts. Next will be the companies that advertise cars, lagers and sportswear during televised games. Viewing figures will decline, as millions realise that they don't really like football that much. Television stations and their allies in high-tech communications will develop new marketing strategies, which do not depend on super-fit young thugs. Apart from a few giants, such as Manchester United, the Premier League clubs will sag into bankruptcy. Meanwhile, beneath them, football will consist of a few part-time clubs.

The fans could stop this. They could boycott matches and cancel their subscriptions to television until football sees sense. They could demand that the billions pouring into the game are shared, so that the smaller teams can survive, providing entertainment and hope for local communities. They could insist that players who behave like yobs are sacked. If fans did this, football would have to listen because without them there is no audience and no money.

Most footballers still come from working-class homes, though the stars of the Premiership live like pop stars or Internet entrepreneurs; even the journeymen of the league, the cloggers and the spoilers who are the bit players in this multimillion pound circus, earn as much as successful accountants, lawyers and private doctors. To become a top-class footballer requires physical strength, ruthlessness and hunger, qualities that are more often found in council estates than detached homes in suburbia. It is a cliché, but a true one, that sport remains the most likely escape for youngsters from households where the only reading material is the *Sun*. At best, the future for these young people is a trade, such as bricklaying or plumbing, or perhaps a job in a factory; at worst it is unemployment or prison. Tennis and golf – and now the newly professionalised rugby union – attract middle-class youngsters but these are exceptions; the bulk of players in the mass sports, football, athletics, boxing, cricket, snooker and so on, left school at sixteen with no qualifications.

But this will change. The parents of a boy who could become an engineer or an architect, earning £50,000 a year, are likely to take a different view of his desire to play football with his friends rather than study when he might be able to make that in a week as a professional footballer. British Asians, who value education more than any section of the community, have been reluctant to allow their children to dedicate themselves to sport but it will not be long before the Premiership is full of young Asian men who would have become dentists or lawyers a few years ago. Clubs once dismissed Afro-Caribbeans as temperamentally and physically unsuited to top-class football and today there is similar prejudice against Asians, but the sport is pragmatic and will forget this nonsense once the first Asian Paul Gascoigne or Michael Owen is discovered.

Imagine that it is the year 2010. Having given up in the United States, where the public, media and advertisers refused to embrace football because it was not played by giants and could not be interrupted every few minutes for commercial breaks, television and the multinationals backed new clubs in the subcontinent, Africa and the Middle East. Now we have the Delhi Eagles, First Calcutta, the Karachi Blues, Lagos City, Johannesburg, Cairo, Beirut United and Tehran. Every major city in the booming countries of the Far East has a first-class team: Beijing, Hong Kong, Nagasaki, Tokyo, Jakarta and Seoul rival the elite clubs of Europe and South America in the strength of their squads and income.

FIFA's World Club Championship, which was dismissed as a waste of time when Manchester United took part in the first one in Brazil in 2000, now rivals UEFA's Champions' League in terms of money-generating power. Like UEFA's competition, the FIFA event sprawls over the year, with qualifying leagues before the knockout phase. Top English clubs, such as Arsenal and Chelsea, crisscross the world in supersonic jets, to China, then India and then on to West Africa, picking up points and earning tens of millions of pounds from television rights and sponsorship deals.

In spring 2000 UEFA and the domestic leagues in Europe proposed that the European Union should legislate to limit the number of foreigners who could play for clubs. They argued that the game was being damaged by the importation of so many players from within the EU and from the rest of the world. Supporters were being alienated by teams that read like a roll call of United Nations' delegates. The development of local players was being threatened; clubs like Chelsea, who needed instant success, did not need to groom young British players when they could buy an international from, say, Italy for a few million pounds or a brilliant Nigerian for the price of an average First Division striker. International football was also being undermined. National managers, especially England's Kevin Keegan, complained that their domestic leagues were dominated by foreigners. Major clubs were also becoming increasingly difficult about releasing players for international duty, which was not surprising since a club like Arsenal saw most of its first team squad disappear whenever internationals were played. But the EU would not – and could not – change the fundamental principle of the community – that EU nationals could work wherever they liked – for the benefit of football. Nor were the major clubs interested; they wanted the best players, and did not care where they came from. It was also pointed out that the plan was unworkable. Would clubs have to cancel the contracts of half their squad to comply with the new regulations limiting them to, say, six overseas players? And if they tried, they would be challenged in the European courts and would lose. Bosman had changed everything and there was nothing that football could do about it.

The new football also required multinational club sides. Most of Manchester United's crowds of 60,000 or so came from the city but the club had millions of fans throughout Britain and the rest of the world. The marketing wizards at Old Trafford argued that it was good business to field a team packed with foreigners, whom the audience could relate to. The same logic applied to clubs everywhere. Television wanted the top Japanese team to include Europeans and South Americans, because viewers in London, Munich and Rio could relate to them.

Sir Stanley Matthews died on Wednesday 23 February 2000, aged eighty-five. The reaction to his death suggested that the country was tiring of football's petulance, arrogance and greed. 'A soccer legend, from the days when players were decent, honest and honourable,' eulogised one newspaper. The same words – 'courteous', 'modest', 'approachable' – occurred in dozens of obituaries, a tribute to Matthews and a condemnation of today's players.

This was a collective pining for the idealised England of Ealing films, policemen on bicycles, back doors left open, fresh bread baking in the oven and children playing happily in the streets. Today is violent, self-obsessed and mercenary; oh, the country sighed, wouldn't it be lovely if we could eliminate all the nastiness of modern life?

This was silly. The past was not Utopia. People had less, worked harder and died earlier. The England that Matthews was born into was tough and unfair. Wages were low. Workers had no rights. The few rich stayed rich and the many poor remained poor.

But these facts were ignored in the wake of his death. He had been a right winger of astonishing speed and guile, and yet had not been spoilt by fame, in contrast with today's stars, most of whom will be forgotten the moment they retire into tax exile.

It is ironic that the country romanticised him like this. He had been modest but also selfish – as all great players are – both on and off the pitch. He had supplemented his weekly football wages in the era of the £20 a week maximum by writing columns and advertising. He even charged for appearing in testimonials. If he had been playing today he would certainly have demanded the same multimillion pound package as David Beckham and it is an insult to his intelligence to suggest otherwise.

Some commentators argued that his remarkable self-discipline and dedication were the result of economic hardship, which today's players never experience. He was born in 1915, the son of a barber in the little Potteries town of Hanley. He made his debut for Stoke when he was seventeen, the start of a playing career that lasted until he was fifty. The statistics are dazzling. He played fifty-four full internationals for England, the last of which was in 1957, when he was forty-two. He was European Footballer of the Year in 1956. He was Footballer of the Year in 1948 and again in 1963, as he edged towards his fiftieth birthday. He is the oldest man to have scored a goal in the league (at forty-eight) and in a cup final (at forty-nine he appeared for Stoke City against Leicester in the two-leg League Cup Final, in the days before it was played at Wcmbley). He was knighted in 1965 before playing his last league match, against Fulhan, aged fifty years and five days.

Would Matthews have carried on for so long if he had been a multimillionaire in his twenties? How would he have coped with today's voracious media? Would he have hidden behind the high-security walls of a mansion? Would the young Matthews prosper today as a player? Most experts who saw him in his prime say that he was magical, without the benefit of modern training, diet and kit, and that he would be irresistible today. But it does not matter whether we know the answers; the mere fact that we ask these questions is a comment on the game. And a warning that the country is beginning to lose patience.

In June 2000 a newspaper sent me to Eindhoven to describe how this prosperous Dutch town, home of the electronics giant Philips, would shortly be sacked by English football hooligans when England opened their Euro 2000 campaign against Portugal.

Although it was only 48 hours before kick-off everything was peaceful, and seemed destined to remain so. The local club, PSV Eindhoven, is Holland's equivalent of Manchester United – so rich and successful that it is universally loathed by Dutch fans – and the police are used to handling belligerent visiting supporters. In the build-up to the match, the British press had caricatured the police here as soft, pot-smokers who would be overwhelmed by the English louts but, as I wandered through the town, it was apparent they were tough and well-organised. One senior officer told me that he was not worried about the English; our Dutch hooligans, he said, are just as vicious and we always cope with them.

There were other factors which suggested that there would not be the major violence predicted by the reporters who were crisscrossing Holland and Belgium, co-hosts of the tournament, in a frantic search for English louts. The match against Portugal was taking place on Monday evening; this was inconvenient for the hooligans, most of whom did not finish work at home until 5.30 pm. Next, the thugs dismissed Portugal as a nothing country: they did not hate it, or even know where it was, and Portugal did not have any fans worth fighting.

Sure enough there was no trouble in Eindhoven, to the disappointment of the British media, which had been anticipating a bloodbath and a great story about the scum who had, yet again, disgraced England. But the match was important for other reasons. Thanks to the only world-class players in the team – David Beckham, Paul Scholes and Steve McManaman – England were soon leading by two goals, but Portugal always looked as if they were going to win, which they did. The Portuguese stroked the ball around and exchanged positions effortlessly; the English, meanwhile, looked as if they had never seen a football before, as it bobbled off their shins or span off their knees, and marched up and down the pitch in formation.

After the first week of Euro 2000 more truths were revealed. The Premiership might be the most exciting league in the world but, if it was, that was because there were so many foreigners in it. Next, it was clear that the old frisson of international football had gone. Once, matches between, say, England and Holland, had an edge, which came from the fact that the opponents were aliens, but here the star players were friends.

Opening matches in a tournament like this had traditionally been tight, grim and bad-tempered, because teams were so desperate not to lose, but the first week of Euro 2000 was a festival of attacking, good-natured football. Watching the goals zip in, it occurred to me that this might be because players no longer cared that much. What did it matter when you were being paid so much by your club in England, Italy, France or Germany?

The British media finally got its hooligan story when England played Germany on a Saturday evening in the scruffy industrial town of Charleroi in southern Belgium. Before a dreadful match between a poor team (England) and a truly awful one (Germany) – won by a header from Alan Shearer, England's ageing, fading striker – English and German hooligans threw punches and chairs at each other in the town square. This skirmish was utterly predictable – the yobs do not work on Saturdays and loathe Germans; the German government had banned many known thugs from travelling but enough were always going to reach Eindhoven to do battle – and provoked the same inquest by the media which always follows appalling behaviour by English fans abroad.

Why does England produce such ghastly creatures: tattooed, racist and irredeemably primitive? Only a few fans had come to Charleroi to cause trouble – and a few hundred more had joined in when it started – but that did not matter. Basic truths – some people are unpleasant; other countries have similar idiots, who seek self-worth through thumping rival supporters; most football supporters are noisy and unattractive but harmless – were forgotten amid the hysteria.

UEFA threatened to expel England if there was further violence, which was fair enough since the presence of a handful of English psychopaths was turning a football tournament into a demonstration of zero-tolerance policing, but it was not necessary. England needed a point from the match against Romania to qualify for the quarter finals but it was obvious within a few minutes that they would be outclassed. Naturally, England lost and were eliminated.

Keegan and his team scuttled home. The players were genuinely surprised by their failure. They had assumed that they were world-beaters because they were paid world-beating salaries, but then they headed off to the sun for a few weeks before beginning pre-season training. Most had probably forgotten Euro 2000 before they had applied the first coating of sun cream: football was just a job and, in any case, the new televison deal meant more money in the Premiership, which, in turn, meant they would be able to demand a pay rise. £25,000 a week was ok if you were just a member of the England squad, but you deserved at least £40,000 if you had actually played.

Television was not happy. The BBC and ITV had just emerged from the auction for the right to show highlights from the Premiership (ITV won, killing the BBC's *Match of the Day* and leaving the corporation with just the FA Cup) and Euro 2000 was a grudge match. The BBC wanted to show that the nation still turned to it for great occasions, sporting or otherwise; ITV was determined to demonstrate that it was the future, and that the BBC belonged to a grey, stuffy past. The BBC team of pundits was led by chirpy Gary Lineker and ITV fielded the wry Des Lynam, supported by ex-England managers, Bobby Robson, Terry Venables and Glenn Hoddle. Both sides knew that everything depended on England: if the team did well, then tens of millions of people, most of whom did not know the difference between a penalty and an indirect free kick, would tune in; if England flopped, however, only real fans would be interested in the fascinating quarter-final clash between Italy and Romania.

Newspapers were simultaneously delighted (catastrophe is more interesting than triumph), furious (who cared about Euro 2000 now?) and puzzled (the millionaires of the Premiership were supposed to be great players). Many thousands of words were devoted to analysing what had gone wrong with English football. The best sports columnists, such as Ian Wooldridge and Jeff Powell, of the *Daily Mail*, pointed out that it was time to accept that these footballers were no better than their predecessors who had earned £20 a week. Foreigners, not Englishmen, were the stars of the Premiership. Neither England nor Germany deserved the 2006 World Cup, which should go to South Africa.

And yet. Newspapers were already cranking up for the 2000–2001 season. Roll up, roll up, they said, and collect your free preview, packed with charts, biographies of the key players and predictions by our experts. Euro 2000 was not over but they were anticipating what really mattered – Arsenal against Chelsea, Manchester United versus Liverpool and so on. Agents and managers were swarming through the Low Countries, leading to 'exclusives' on the back pages of the tabloids about top Europeans who would be coming to the Premiership on four year deals worth £50,000 a week.

The show rolls on, louder, richer and more arrogant than ever. Only the fans can force the industry that is football today to come to its senses. It is up to them.

Bibliography and Sources

There are many excellent books on football – descriptive, reportage, autobiographical and wholly factual – and I have drawn extensively from them. I am especially indebted to Dominic Hobson for his masterly survey of sport in his study, *The National Wealth: Who Gets What in Britain*. Descriptive books, such as Pete Davies' *All Played Out*, an account of the 1990 World Cup, gave me valuable insights. Autobiographies, such as Harry Redknapp's hilarious book, helped me understand the old and new footballs. Reportage, such as Hunter Davies' *The Glory Game* and Dan Goldstein's penetrating accounts of the 92 league clubs in English Football, *The Rough Guide*, provided facts and anecdotes. I am grateful to all these authors. I would also like to acknowledge my debt to the country's football journalists whose work is always enjoyable and often revealing.

European Football: The Rough Guide by Peterjon Cresswell and Simon Evans (The Rough Guides, 1999)

The Glory Game by Hunter Davies (Mainstream, 1972 & 1996)

All Played Out by Pete Davies (William Heinemann, 1990)

Only a Game? by Eamon Dunphy (Viking, 1976 & Penguin 1987)

'Arry: The Autobiography of Harry Redknapp by Harry Redknapp (CollinsWillow, 1998)

Staying Up: A fan behind the scenes in the Premiership by Rick Gekoski (Warner Books, 1999)

Playing at Home by John Aizlewood (Orion, 1998)

4 – 2 by David Thompson (Bloomsbury, 1996)

Fever Pitch by Nick Hornby (Victor Gollancz, 1992)

The National Wealth: Who Gets What in Britain by Dominic Hobson (HarperCollins, 1999)

Alex Ferguson, Managing My Life: My Autobiography by Alex Ferguson with Hugh McIlvanney (Hodder and Stoughton, 1999)

Own Goal!

The Second Most Important Job in the Country by Niall Edworthy (Virgin Publishing, 1999)

Kicking with Both Feet by Frank Clark (Headline, 2000)

Football Confidential by Ian Bent, Richard McIlroy, Kevin Mousley and Peter Walsh (BBC Worldwide, 2000)

Red Voices by Stephen F Kelly (Headline, 2000)

Manchester United: The complete fact book by Michael Crick (Profile Books, 1999)

The Journalists by Arnold Wesker (Jonathan Cape, 1979)

Journey into Journalism by Arnold Wesker (Writers and Readers Publishing Cooperative, 1977)

Vinnie: The Autobiography, Confessions of a Bad Boy? by Vinnie Jones (Headline, 1998)

Addicted by Tony Adams (CollinsWillow, 1998)

English Football: A Fan's Handbook, 1999 – 2000 by Dan Golstein (The Rough Guides, 1999)

Left Foot Forward by Garry Nelson (Headline, 1995)

Rothman's Football Yearbook, 1999-2000 edited by Glenda Rollin & Jack Rollin (Headline, 1999)

Manslaughter United: A season with a Prison Football Team by Chris Hulme (Yellow Jersey Press, 1999)

Derby Days: The games we love to hate by Dougie and Eddy Brimson (Headline, 1998)

Playfair Football Annual 1999-2000 edited by Glenda Rollin (Headline, 1999)

Football Yearbook 1999-2000, Carling Opta (Carlton Books, 1999)

For Love or Money by Alex Flynn and Lynton Guest (Andre Deutsch, 1999)

Football by Chris Nawrat (Icon Books, 1998)

Fergie: The biography of Alex Ferguson by Stephen F Kelly (Headline, 1997)

Don't Shoot The Manager by Jimmy Greaves with Norman Giller (Boxtree, 1993)

Football and its Fans, 1885 – 1985 by Rogan Taylor (Leicester University Press, 1992)

Hooligans Abroad by John Williams, Eric Dunning & Patrick Murphy (Routledge & Kegan Paul, 1984)

Bibliography and Sources

Black Sportsmen by Ernest Cashmore (Routledge & Kegan Paul, 1982)

We Hate Humans by Dave Robins (Penguin, 1984)

Success in Football by Mike Smith (John Murray, 1973)

Beginner's Guide to Soccer Training and Coaching by Brian Owen with Nigel Clarke (Pelham Books, 1973)

Good Times, Bad Times by Harold Evans (Weidenfeld and Nicolson, 1983)

British Society Since 1945 by Arthur Marwick (Penguin, 1982)

British Society 1914 – 1945 by John Stevenson (Penguin, 1984)

Britain in the Nineteen Thirties by Noreen Branson and Margot Heinemann (Granada, 1973)

Index

Index

Index